Advance Praise for
Million-Dollar Moments

In my graduate studies at the School at the Art Institute of Chicago, and in university classrooms where I have taught, I was only one of a few that had professional experience in these areas (development/advancement/fundraising and those studying to work and lead nonprofits). It was evident that for those who didn't have much experience, the concept of philanthropy and fundraising was not easy for them to incorporate into their advanced studies and budding careers, whether they intended to practice in, or provide services for, the nonprofit arena. This book is a valuable tool for stimulating conversations and awareness that will deepen these individuals' abilities to recognize, understand, and cause transformative moments in their own work.

Gail Sheil
Million-Dollar Donor and former Board Chair,
Damar Services, Inc.

Rick has done a masterful job of providing rich insight and great context surrounding the making of major philanthropic gifts. There are so many fascinating, compelling, and provocative human thoughts and dynamics surrounding million dollar gifts, and this book has helped lift these dynamics to the surface for the reader's easy consumption. While this is not designed to serve as a "how to" book, it unequivocally educates, enlightens, and gives invaluable counsel to the reader. If you can read this book without gaining profound insight into how you might more effectively cultivate a major gift, then you have not read the book.

Dennis E. Bland, Esq.
President and CEO, Center for
Leadership Development

The act of listening and learning about a donor's philanthropic passions is an art. A million dollar gift is not cultivated overnight; it is a combination of time, trust, and collaboration between the donor, gift officer, and recipient. Rick demonstrates the art of philanthropy by taking the reader on this journey and highlighting how one's passion can transform an individual, family, or community. This book will not only inspire you, it will bring lasting smiles knowing that you, too, were part of an act of kindness that helped create positive change.

Lisa Nierenberg
President, BlueRiver Philanthropy, and
Development Director, SeriesFest

MILLION-DOLLAR MOMENTS:
And the Amazing Professionals
Who Made Them Possible

By Rick Markoff

Foreword by Denise DeBartolo York

The University of Toledo Press

The University of Toledo Press
www.utoledopress.com

Copyright 2018
By the University of Toledo Press

Million-Dollar Moments:
And the Amazing Professionals Who Made Them Possible

Edited by Yarko Kuk

Book Design by Stephanie Delo

Cover Design by Steve Markoff and Cory Stevens

Project assistance from Erin Czerniak, Beau Case, and Celia Daniels

ISBN 978-0-692-16307-8

Dedication

For my father, Jack Hy Markoff, the most remarkable salesman I have
ever known. For Don Rizzo, the finest example of a resource development
professional I have ever met. And for Byron Tweeten, the master of
organizational reinvention, process redesign, and major philanthropy.

Table of Contents

Foreword

By Denise DeBartolo York

As the son of Italian immigrants, my father, Edward J. DeBartolo, Sr., grew up with the belief that family was of the utmost importance. To my father, however, our family extended far beyond the confines of our home or our bloodline.

My father learned the importance of education at an early age. In grade school, he witnessed how difficult it was for his father to bid construction projects due to the language barrier. He often had to step in to assist, and ended up teaching his parents DeBartolo York English. His father's inability to communicate on the same level as his competitors hindered the family's ability to enjoy the life in America of which they dreamed.

More than six decades ago, my father set a tremendous example for my siblings and me when he established the Italian Scholarship League in our hometown of Youngstown, Ohio. He always stressed the importance of our own education, but now he had taken it upon himself to help provide for the education of our community. My father's passion for education was born of his own life experiences, and his desire to help others even their own "playing fields" continues to live on today through me, my family, and the San Francisco 49ers.

Today, the 49ers Foundation, the nonprofit community funding extension of the San Francisco 49ers, is the embodiment of my father's legacy as a philanthropist and community citizen. I know my father would be extremely proud of our efforts, as the 49ers Foundation has been internationally recognized as one of the most impactful in all of sports, having recently been named the 2017 ESPN Sports Humanitarian Team of the Year. The 49ers were also named Beyond Sport's 2015 Sport Team of the Year for Outstanding Philanthropic

Sports Organization and the 2013 winner of the prestigious Robert Wood Johnson Foundation Steve Patterson Award for Sports Philanthropy.

The 49ers Foundation focuses much of its efforts on improving the lives of at-risk youth, while leveraging education as a core vehicle to progress. In 2014, we launched two educational initiatives designed to make a long-lasting impact for youth throughout the Bay Area. The 49ers STEAM Education Program at Levi's Stadium and The 49ers STEM Leadership Institute at Cabrillo Middle School and Santa Clara High School help the youth of our region excel in the curriculum of science, technology, engineering, art, and mathematics. These programs are just a few that have directly benefitted from the more than $40 million contributed by the 49ers Foundation in support of nonprofits since 1992.

As an individual whose philanthropic values were instilled at such a young age, I continue to be inspired by the stories of others with similar interests who endeavor to improve the lives of others. Our world continues to flourish, spurred on by innovation, and in the same way, we must find better ways to live our lives and positively affect the lives of others. There is so much to be gained from the touching stories collected by Rick Markoff in *Million-Dollar Moments.*

Roughly 10 years ago, I was on the board of Simon Property Group and came into contact with Rick. He was so bright and hardworking, and his desire to advocate for youth was quite impressive. I learned a great many things about Rick from observing his demeanor and the diligence he displayed in regularly checking in on the Simon Youth Academies in Simon's various malls. During his visits to the Southern Park Mall, located in Youngstown across from my corporate office, we would regularly get together. From there we developed a relationship built around our shared passion for community involvement, in particular for children and young adults. Each spring, I look forward to sharing with Rick my excitement as we watch the young people we have worked with reach their goals. Graduation day is so very special to us.

It is days such as those that make our philanthropic efforts worthwhile and rewarding. I am very grateful for Rick's work in detailing the experiences and lessons learned by resource development professionals and nonprofit executives who have seen firsthand the transformational impact major gifts can have on an organization and the individuals it serves.

This book is a tremendous resource for everyone associated with the world of philanthropy—donors, recipients, volunteers, educators and anyone who cares about positively impacting the lives of others. As Rick shares with the reader, a million-dollar story focuses on the connection made between an institution or cause that resonates deeply with the values of a person with means. Through the eyes of the recipient, we are able to see the true impact these memorable gifts have on nonprofit organizations and those they serve.

We are so lucky that Rick has chosen to share his wisdom of more than four decades in philanthropy with the world.

Acknowledgements

It is said that there is a book in all of us. However, I did not have the time, energy, perspective, and volume of experience to write *Million-Dollar Moments* until my retirement in 2016. I'm glad I waited.

Just like the process that made so many million-dollar moments happen, there was a need, a team, a progression, an impact, and a series of lessons learned from this venture.

The book tells the stories of eighteen resource development professionals and nonprofit leaders: who they are, how they made their career choices, and the hoops they went through to become resource development and nonprofit professionals. More importantly, this is a book about their first million-dollar gifts or their most significant million-dollar gifts...how these gifts came about, what these gifts meant to the organizations represented by said professionals, and the lessons learned throughout the process. It is not a "how to" resource, and it is not written from the perspective of the contributor or donor. It is about professionalism, team, process, personalization, and relationships... major building blocks of the best resource development programs.

Because I was an unknown quantity as an author, numerous people had to take a chance on me: Andrea Neely, Byron Tweeten, Colette Murray, Danny Dean, Dee Metaj, Dennis Stefanacci, Frank Habib, Gene Tempel, John Lore, Karen Burns, Kathy Carroll, Ken Gladish, Mark Helmus, Ruth Johnson, Scott Evenbeck, Sharon Pierce, Steve Helmich, and Vance Peterson. They represent the best of the best in the profession and were a pleasure to work with as contributors of *Million-Dollar Moments* chapters.

The final chapter, Concluding Thoughts, captures the impact of *Million-Dollar Moments* from a full complement the best and the brightest resource development and nonprofit professionals across the country: Ann Murtlow, Beverley Pitts, Curt Simic, Dan Saevig, Jacquie Ackerman, Jon Labahn, Ken File, Sam Kennedy, Sheri Gladden, Trish Oman Clark, and Una Osili. From those who have recently entered the field to those who have spent a lifetime of mission fulfillment, they offer a unique insight into the impact of meaningful gifts.

Two individuals who provided me with valuable research for the book were David C. Hammack and Tom Schweizer. Andy Klein, Larry Leaman, Larry Morwick, and Joanne Ollivier made proofreading much easier.

I am so proud that my dear friend Denise DeBartolo York, owner of the San Francisco 49ers and highly respected business leader, wrote the Foreword to *Million-Dollar Moments*. Other key endorsements came from Charles Bantz, Dennis Bland, Ed Bonach, Lisa Nierenberg, Ora Pescovitz, Gail Sheil, and Dan Smith.

All of their efforts would have gone by the wayside if the right publisher weren't found. I am so fortunate that the publisher was The University of Toledo Press. The Press' belief in the subject matter, and in me, meant so much to the credibility of the endeavor. I can't thank Editor Yarko Kuk enough.

As a first-time author, I sought out the assistance of those who understood the field and who shared their knowledge with me. I benefited from the expertise of Patti Beach, Sandra Markle, David Rosenbaum, Fred Sievert, Leah Stern, and Lilya Wagner.

On a more personal note, great credit goes to the women and men who serve our nation's nonprofits and their missions…from rural communities to crowded urban cities, from the arts and humanities to STEM, from cures to computers, from research to women's rights, from the pulpit to animal preservation, and from agriculture to outer space…I thank the nation's servant leaders.

I have been blessed with great education, opportunity, mentors, and family. Without this combination, there would not be a *Million-Dollar Moments*.

My alma maters include Fostoria High School, Western Michigan University, University of Missouri, the University of Toledo, and the United States Army.

The nonprofits which gave me the opportunity to serve others as a paid executive include: Western Michigan University, Adrian College, St. Vincent Medical Center Foundation, STAR Alliance, Simon Youth Foundation, Indiana University-Purdue University Indianapolis, and Damar Services and Foundation. Just as importantly, any success I attained came in tandem with my fellow associates, leaders, directors and trustees, donors, grantors, guild and auxiliary members, volunteers, and friends.

Equally meaningful was the education I received from leading nonprofits in a volunteer capacity. My work with Congregation Etz Chayim, the National Society of Fundraising Executives, Sylvania (Ohio) City Schools, Congregation Shaarey Tefilla, and the Indiana University School of Nursing Advisory Board all had a lasting impression.

My mentors were Grandfather Myer Shiff, teacher Dorothy Link, coaches Douglas Thompson and Carlos Jackson, Western Michigan University senior class advisor John Lore, Rotarian Danny Danielson, and IUPUI Chancellor Charles Bantz.

What can I say about family that doesn't sound trite? Mom and Dad, Mamie Carolyn and Jack Markoff, provided me with unlimited options to become the best person I could be. My wife, Beverly Markoff, has been by my side since July 30, 1972. She has shown me the love, interjected the confidence, and given me the support to complete this endeavor and every other major endeavor I have tackled. Older son Steve masterminded the book's artwork and design, while younger son, Matt, was my legal advisor.

To those in my profession, and those who make *Million-Dollar Moments* possible across our great country, I share with you the words of Katrina Mayer, author of *The Mustard Seed Way*: "At the end of the day, the only questions I will ask myself are…Did I love enough? Did I laugh enough? Did I make a difference?"

CHAPTER ONE
Genevieve Haugh Aldham Christ
By Rick Markoff

As I set out on my journey to write *Million-Dollar Moments*, I felt three questions were necessary to ask and answer: Why is a million dollar gift so meaningful? What is the history of million-dollar gifts in the United States? and Who really receives million-dollar gifts in the United States?

To understand my interest in the magic of a million-dollar gift, allow me to tell you about my first million-dollar moment. Late in June, 1986, I received a phone call from Joe Murphy, Vice President of the Morton Plant Hospital Foundation, Clearwater, Florida. Joe, the consummate resource development professional, and I had built a friendship over the previous two years, stemming from a relationship with a mutual donor, Genevieve Haugh Aldham Christ. I was President of the St. Vincent Medical Center Foundation, a post I held for more than a decade.

Joe told me Genevieve had passed away earlier in the week, and that Morton Plant Hospital Foundation and St. Vincent Medical Center Foundation would be two of four major beneficiaries of her estate. The minimum amount each organization would receive was $1 million.

A 1927 graduate of the St. Vincent Hospital School of Nursing, Genevieve became an important major gift contributor to Morton Plant while she lived in Largo, Florida. I still remember a St. Vincent volunteer, Helen Schaal, a classmate of Genevieve's, walking into my office in early 1985 to share with me a Tampa newspaper article announcing a one million dollar gift Genevieve had made to Morton Plant. It was the impetus for Morton Plant Hospital to build the Aldham-Christ Day Surgery Center at a cost of $3.5 million.

Not long after her generous 1984 gift to the Florida hospital, Genevieve came to Toledo to visit relatives. Arrangements were made for her to meet with St. Vincent President, Allen Johnson, and me.

Several weeks later, I received an invitation from Genevieve to attend the Aldham-Christ Day Surgery Center ribbon-cutting. Surrounded by family, friends, and Morton Plant executives, Genevieve went out of her way to make me feel welcome. She even had me join her family afterward for a wonderful luncheon.

Million-dollar gifts in the mid-1980s generated a great deal of attention in the media. The bulk of Genevieve's estate came from T. Edward Aldham. Mr. Aldham was a chemist, and with his partner, Frederick Franklin, developed the FRAM oil filter, an item used in millions of automobiles. The FRAM name came from the FR in Franklin and the AM in Aldham. The two men amassed their fortune in Providence, Rhode Island from the oil filter and other automobile engine parts.

Genevieve was family-oriented and loved her four brothers and sisters and eleven nieces and nephews. Although she married several times, she had no children. Genevieve outlived each of her husbands.

Prior to her passing, Genevieve and I met three more times. One of these meetings included a tour of updated St. Vincent Medical Center and School of Nursing facilities, followed by lunch with Toledo business leader and St. Vincent supporter Virgil Gladieux. Genevieve and Virgil got along famously. Virgil's experience in cultivating a relationship with Genevieve would later help influence and energize fellow members of the St. Vincent Foundation Board of Trustees to become active participants in securing additional major gifts for a $10 million capital campaign.

We developed the "Design for Leadership" campaign to maintain and assure St. Vincent Medical Center's financial ability to deliver quality care for the poor and needy. At the same time, we wanted to provide a guarantee for the preservation of its centers of excellence. In a world of decreasing business and government support, volunteer leadership felt it was important to ensure the greater Toledo region continued to receive the desperately needed nursing professional care that was in an increasingly short supply. At the time "Design for Leadership" was implemented, St. Vincent, a 621-bed facility serving the underserved and underinsured of northwest Ohio and southeast

Michigan, was sponsored and operated by the Sisters of Charity of Montreal, the Grey Nuns. "Design for Leadership" was a vital element in achieving the much sought-after stability.

Genevieve died after a prolonged battle with cancer. Even in her final days filled with illness and pain, she asked me to visit her at her condominium to clarify some of the details of her will. Genevieve knew her life was ending, and she wanted to make clear her intentions to include the St. Vincent Hospital and Medical Center Foundation in her will. I would discover in the months to come that each time we met, Genevieve either wrote the St. Vincent Medical Center Foundation into her will, or would add a codicil amending the document. Our meetings, lunch with Virgil Gladieux, and her strong Catholic faith definitely had an impact on Genevieve's outlook in her waning days.

Two memories are clear in my mind as I look back upon receipt of the gift from Genevieve. First, the American economy was in recession for much of the time she and I developed our relationship. However, the economy rebounded, and through some excellent decision-making based on sound legal advice, along with the sale of Genevieve's condominium, the million dollars grew to $1,769,000 before the Foundation received its final payment. Second, the bequest would serve as the key leadership gift in the three-year, $10 million capital campaign the Foundation Board of Trustees had approved. "Design for Leadership" provided $12.5 million to the Medical Center, $2.5 million beyond its goal.

Newly appointed St. Vincent Medical Center President, Larry Leaman, and I, along with our fundraising consultants at Growth Design Corporation, Milwaukee, decided to keep the announcement a surprise until the September 22, 1987, meeting of the St. Vincent Medical Center Foundation Board of Directors. We felt the Board would be ecstatic. Instead, the achievement was overshadowed by an announcement earlier in the day that U.S. Navy helicopters sank an Iranian ship in the Persian Gulf. While the Board's 40 business executives, physicians, and community leaders were happy to receive the Foundation's first million-dollar gift, their hearts were heavy with concern for our nation's welfare.

Many of the lessons to be learned from Genevieve's million-dollar moment will be mentioned frequently by other contributors throughout this book, but two remain prominent to both her life and her gift.

Resource development professionals and nonprofit leaders have the ability to build and enhance powerful relationships with individuals and entities which cause life-changing events to occur. Educations are made possible. Lives are saved. The arts are shared. The environment and ecosystems are shared and protected. History is preserved. Research is conducted. Heartstrings are touched.

Understand the importance of your organization's mission. Appreciate the power your position has to help direct the destiny of that organization. Maximize your ability to bring other professionals and volunteers into the process to cultivate potential donors and effectively tell the organization's story. Above all else, treasure and protect the relationships you build with every donor. You always represent their interests, their hopes and dreams, and their passion to do good, to affect change, to be there for others, and to serve others before self.

The second lesson I learned in the resource development process is you can't judge a book by its cover. In the nearly 60 years from the time Genevieve graduated from the St. Vincent School of Nursing until she passed away, she made two gifts to her alma mater's development fund and foundation. Each of those gifts was $200. They were, by no means, indicators of her financial capabilities, nor her deep-rooted love for St. Vincent.

All too often, resource development professionals look for the most expedient use of their time to produce numbers for the bottom line. Instead, understand you have to put in the work. The resource development cycle includes identification, cultivation, education, activation and motivation, solicitation, celebration and recognition, communication, and evaluation of this process over and over again. There are no short cuts. When success is achieved, let others take the bow. That is what good resource development is all about.

Genevieve provided the first of four million-dollar gifts in which I participated during my career. Each one was exciting, was a difference-maker to the organization, was a great sense of pride to the three individual contributors and one organizational contributor, and, in each instance, was the culmination of a team effort. The professionals and volunteers involved in all four gifts were completely dedicated to the mission of their organization and put the best interests of the team ahead of individual goals and objectives.

The million-dollar gift has sizzle. It is attention-getting. It is often news worthy. It is the dream of many philanthropically-bent individuals to make such a commitment. It is often the gift which creates the momentum, or brings to a successful completion, a major need or a capital campaign for the vast majority of American nonprofits.

About Richard (Rick) M. Markoff, PhD

Markoff

Richard M. Markoff retired on December 31, 2015 after serving eighteen months as the Founding President of the Damar Foundation. The Foundation raises funds to support the work of Damar Services, which has been serving children and adults challenged by autism and intellectual, developmental, and behavioral disabilities for more than 50 years.

Before coming to the Damar Foundation, in 2011, Rick coordinated the Central Indiana Education Alliance as the former Visiting Senior Advisor to Chancellor Charles R. Bantz and taught Organizational Leadership graduate courses as Visiting Lecturer for the School of Engineering and Technology, Indiana University Purdue University Indianapolis.

He served as Executive Vice President of the Simon Youth Foundation (SYF), from 2002 to 2010. Simon Property Group, Inc. is the world's largest shopping mall owner and operator. A nationally recognized leader in alternative education, SYF was selected the 2008 recipient of the Education Commission of the States' Corporate Award. Previous winners included Hewlett Packard, Intel, MBNA, PBS, and Washington Mutual. The National Dropout Prevention Center/Network presented SYF with its Crystal Star Award in 2008 and named SYF an Exemplary Program in 2009. The International Council of Shopping Centers Foundation bestowed upon SYF its US Community Support Award, and prestigious Albert Sussman International Community Support Award. The Mutual of America Foundation announced SYF was a 2010 recipient of a Community Partnership Award.

Under Dr. Markoff's leadership, SYF, in collaboration with its public school and higher education partners, established 25 Education Resource Centers—schools in malls—in twelve states. The centers which have a 90 percent graduation rate and serve 3,300 at-risk and economically challenged youth on a daily basis. In addition, SYF awarded more than $4.2 million in scholarships during Fiscal Years 2008, 2009, and 2010.

Preceding his arrival at SYF, Dr. Markoff was in the Office of the CEO, Government and Community Relations, for the American Red Cross of Greater Indianapolis, where he initiated and successfully completed the merger of STAR Alliance into the Red Cross. During Dr. Markoff's Presidency from 1995 to 2001, STAR Alliance was responsible for one of the most effective and comprehensive substance abuse prevention programs in the United States.

Prior to moving to Indianapolis in 1995, Dr. Markoff was President of the St. Vincent Medical Center Foundation in Toledo, from 1983 to 1994. While in Toledo, he was Founding President of the Greater Toledo Chapter of the National Society of Fundraising Executives, President of the Sylvania, Ohio, City Schools Board of Education, and President of the Congregation Etz Chayim Board of Directors. His community service continued in Indianapolis where he was President of Congregation Shaarey Tefilla, and served on the American Red Cross of Greater Indianapolis, the Rotary Club of Indianapolis, and the Indiana Chapter of the Association of Fundraising Professionals Boards of Directors. A former member of Indiana University (IU) Hospital's Melvin and Bren Simon Cancer Center Development Board, Dr. Markoff was appointed Chair of the IU School of Nursing Advisory

Board February 1, 2016, serving in that capacity through March, 2017.

A native of Fostoria, Ohio, Dr. Markoff holds degrees from Western Michigan University (BA, 1968), the University of Missouri-Columbia (MEd, 1970) and the University of Toledo (PhD, 1978). Rick was elected President of Western's Class of 1968. As a Field Artillery officer in the United States Army, he was awarded the Bronze Star and Vietnam Cross of Gallantry with Palm. The former Western Michigan University and Adrian College administrator was recognized by the University of Toledo College of Education in 2008 with its Distinguished Achievement Award. Dr. Markoff has spoken at more than 50 high school graduations across the country. He was featured in the May-June 2010 issue of Advancing Philanthropy.

Dr. Markoff is married to Beverly, an award-winning interior designer. They have two sons, Steve, of Carmel, Indiana, and Matthew, of Sherman Oaks, California. Both sons are employed in the music industry. Steve is Creative Director for Live Nation, Indianapolis and Hollywood, and Matt is President of Holy Toledo Productions.

CHAPTER TWO

IBM and Dr. Robert I. Sinsheimer

By Colette M. Murray

While I was serving as the legal counsel for the Berkeley campus, I was recruited to run the California Alumni Association. As legal counsel, I established the UC Berkeley Foundation. The current CEO of the alumni association was recruited to head the foundation. I then moved into the alumni position which I held for five or six years. I was then recruited by University of California, Santa Cruz (UCSC). My charge was three-fold: to set up their foundation, to create a full-service development program, and to expand the alumni program. It was certainly a higher level positon and a great challenge, not to mention a fabulous area.

In the late 1970s and early 1980s, the entering students at UCSC had the highest math scores in the country. Dr. Robert L. Sinsheimer, who was named Chancellor in 1977, was a visionary who appreciated and understood the profile of the student body. At the time, he was the editor of *Science Magazine*. Among other accomplishments, he was the creator of the single strand DNA virus. He was also one of the first scientists to propose and seriously consider that a concerted effort be undertaken to sequence the human genome. Dr. Sinsheimer received numerous awards and honors for his achievements. He was named California Scientist of the Year in 1968 and authored some 200 publications in his various areas of research interest.

Dr. Sinsheimer was involved in writing a new academic plan for the campus, and among other innovations, he instituted a requirement that no student could graduate unless he or she was "computer literate," which was, perhaps, the first institution of higher education with such a provision.

As the first person to be appointed a full-time exccutive overseeing all advancement operations, and with an emphasis on fundraising, I arrived on campus on July 1, 1978, as Assistant Chancellor for University Relations. Since UCSC was a very young campus—the first class of undergraduates was 1968, I realized we needed to focus on non-alumni for major philanthropic gifts, including major corporations. Although UCSC was not literally in the shadow of the Silicon Valley, we were close. In light of the fact Chancellor Sinsheimer had recently created a new undergraduate major in computer engineering, the logical next step was for us to explore partnering with some of the major organizations in the emerging high-tech/bio-tech neighbor to the North.

One of the early giants in Silicon Valley was IBM; therefore, it made sense to start with arranging a visit with their program officers. Because of the international reputation of Dr. Sinsheimer, it was relatively easy to obtain an initial appointment.

In early 1979, we met with a senior officer, which was the beginning of a two-plus-year process which ended in a priceless, one of a kind gift to the University. It possibly has never been replicated anywhere since. While we were exploring possible partnerships, the IBM Personal Computer was introduced in August of 1981. A few months after that, IBM agreed to donate PCs to every UCSC student—7,500 in total—as well as most of the members of the faculty. Interestingly enough, the students and faculty at UCSC actually had PCs before some of the IBM staff.

One of the most memorable days in my career was the day the first trucks sporting the IBM logos arrived from San José. As they entered the campus and headed up the long incline to "the campus on the hill," it was quite a sight. As one can imagine, the gift made a phenomenal impact on not just the campus in general but on each recipient, specifically. This was a life changing moment for so many, possibly more valuable than a million-dollar moment, if thinking collectively on the future impact those students would make.

The most important lesson I learned from the IBM experience is that, no matter how skilled I was as a fundraising professional, my job was to not be "numero uno." I was always involved, but I made sure Dr. Sinsheimer and a couple of professors of computer engineering were front and center throughout the process. I urge you to Google Dr. Sinsheimer and read his obituary. He was an amazing man.

Epilogue: After his tenure at UCSC, Dr. Sinsheimer joined the faculty at University of California, Santa Barbara, and although he retired in 1990, he remained active in laboratory research for many years. His autobiography, *The Strands of a Life: The Science of DNA and the Art of Education*, was published in 1994. Dr. Sinsheimer passed away on April 24, 2017 at age 97.

About Colette M. Murray, JD, CFRE.

Colette M. Murray is the Chief Executive Officer of Paschal-Murray, a specialized executive search firm with offices in Wilmington, North Carolina and San Diego, California. She has over 35 years experience in senior level advancement at major higher education and health institutions throughout the country.

A native of California, Colette is a graduate of the University of California, Berkeley. She has a law degree from the

Murray

University of San Francisco, and was in private practice in the San Francisco Bay Area before being appointed the first legal counsel for the UC Berkeley campus. Her career in institutional advancement began with appointment as Executive Director of the California Alumni Association and continued at UC Santa Cruz where she was Vice Chancellor for University Relations.

In 1985, she accepted the position of Vice President for Development and Alumni Affairs at the University of Louisville, and, in 1988, she was named Vice President for Development and University Relations for Texas Tech University and Health Sciences Center. Her history with implementing a department turn-around and stewarding advancement operations into compliance, efficiency, and fund income through role model production was a hallmark of her brand.

Colette is Past Chair of the Association of Fundraising Professionals

(AFP) and Past Chair of the AFP Ethics Committee. She is also past Chair of Council for the Advancement and Support of Education (CASE) and served on the Association for Healthcare Philanthropy (AHP) Board. She has served on over thirty nonprofit boards, including the boards of Leadership California, Leadership America, and LEAD San Diego, the Oakland Symphony, the San Diego Performing Arts League, the YWCA of San Diego County, the boards of AFP Detroit, AFP San Diego, and the AFP Triangle Chapter. She is also a past-president of the San Diego Downtown Breakfast Rotary Club. In addition, she has been named an Outstanding Fundraising Professional in Detroit, San Diego, and the Desert Communities of California.

Colette has won numerous awards, with her most treasured being the first recipient of the Father Hesburgh Award for her service to CASE. Father Hesburgh was the President of Notre Dame for 35 years.

Colette is married to Richard Murray. The pair are co-owners of Paschal-Murray, Executive Search. Colette has managed nearly 600 search projects for positions in institutional advancement—more than any living person today. They have a daughter, Thea Kano, a musician and conductor performing regularly in New York City, Washington, D.C., and Paris.

CHAPTER THREE
It Was All About Education
By Andrea Neely

The path to my million-dollar moment started years ago, even before my professional career began, when my mother told me, "Pay it forward by giving back, no matter how small."

I grew up in Indianapolis and was part of the last graduating class from Shortridge High School in the 1980s. When I completed my diploma in three years, I had just turned 17. After attending Indiana University-Purdue University Indianapolis on a part-time basis, I transferred to Indiana University in Bloomington where I majored in Public Affairs.

After college, I began my career in banking from working in mortgages in the secondary market to supporting credit analysis on commercial real estate loans. Six years later, with the change in banking to focus on the Community Reinvestment Act (CRA), I transitioned into a role that focused on economic development with Near North Community Development Corporation, developing affordable housing opportunities for low income families and communities with a high demand. Over the next six years, I led development programs as a Program Administrator for Near North and as Director of Economic Development with Community Action of Greater Indianapolis. Economic development was the major emphasis of my leadership role within both organizations.

My passion to have a greater impact on the lives of the families that resembled mine in communities across Indianapolis and throughout the state of Indiana energized me to launch my own economic development consulting firm, Paige's Inc., in the late 1990s. It gave me great pleasure knowing I was making a real difference in the lives of others. Over the next ten years, my firm would raise more than $10 million to develop programs and projects that assisted low-income families and seniors with safe, affordable housing. It was enough of an impact that President George W. Bush recognized the firm's efforts during the Indiana Black Expo Corporate Luncheon for its role in developing affordable housing for Indianapolis seniors through the local Housing and Urban Development (HUD) office. In addition, I was acknowledged as the first female consultant to be awarded a HUD grant of $4.1 million on its first submission for developing a 50-unit affordable housing project for seniors—a project that was completed on time and under budget.

As I worked within the community, I saw that for low-income families, education was the key to rise above the status they were often mired in for generations. I wanted to do something that helped break the cycle of poverty, and the same community foundations which helped our consulting firm be impactful in housing were also major players in the field of education. After ten years in economic development, I was asked to join an organization whose specialty was helping students of color earn college degrees. It was here that I felt a difference could be made for future generations, opening education options beyond grade twelve.

The organization in question was the United Negro College Fund (UNCF), an association of 37 historically black colleges and universities (HBCUs). For more than seven decades, the principle "a mind is a terrible thing to waste" has remained at the heart of UNCF, enabling us to raise more than $4.7 billion and help more than 445,000 students and counting graduate from college, thrive, and become leaders. Since our founding in 1944, UNCF helped to more than double the number of minorities attending college. In 2014, the six-year graduation rate for UNCF African-American scholarship recipients was 70 percent, 11 percentage points higher than the national average, and 31 percentage points higher than the national average for African-Americans.

I was on the path to my transformational million-dollar moment, following my mother's teaching, paying it forward by giving back, fulfilling the mission of an organization that can change the lives of future generations.

Working for a national organization that was established to help bright students reach their dreams of a college education has been life-changing for me, and for the students who have been assisted. Over

$68 million has been raised from the State of Indiana for UNCF during my eleven year tenure, making a difference in the lives of many. It has been a privilege to learn from the best and brightest minds throughout Indiana in a joint effort to develop strategies to grow resources and options for students who need help. Our leadership councils consist of leaders from each community, influential heads of key corporations, foundations, churches, clubs and organizations, in addition to civic leaders who work diligently from Fort Wayne to Evansville, and Indianapolis to Gary, in support of the mission of UNCF.

Much of my work involves building relationships and partnerships to develop programs that help students from across the country not only go to school but to complete their degrees and transition into the workforce. These programs provide scholarships and paid internships which help students reduce their debt burdens.

But my colleagues and I realized that helping students graduate from college could not be the end of our mission. Most students go to college to find careers to support their families and their communities. Internships help provide the work experiences needed to obtain a job upon graduation. Too often, however, students do not select majors that would prepare them for careers which are in high demand. While they earn a degree, they are left with debt and few job opportunities.

This was understood by Clarence Crain, Program Director of Lilly Endowment Inc. (LEI), a long-time partner with whom I have had the pleasure of working for more than eight years. Together, we explored programs and opportunities that would help students who wanted to attend HBCUs or Indiana state schools through matching grants. In addition, we examined programs that assisted students who attended community colleges, and sought to complete baccalaureate degrees at four-year institutions. This partnership aimed for more than increasing the rate of students going to college. It was imperative our efforts increased the chances of students graduating from college and reduced their debt for attending college. Degree attainment often came with great debt. The situation was even worse if the newly minted degree recipients had majors which were not in demand within the work force.

Along with other senior leadership of LEI, Clarence Crain saw the impact that UNCF's pioneering Institute for Capacity Building (ICB) had on helping UNCF's 37 HBCUs increase the numbers of minorities who sought education beyond grade twelve, and successfully traversed the system to graduate. The ICB enabled UNCF member HBCUs be financially prepared to put needed programs in place and to recruit the right faculty for colleges and universities. Clarence and I would often discuss how LEI could enhance UNCF effectiveness. We further contemplated what the structure of such a partnership could be.

Clarence, senior leadership of LEI, and I became part of a much larger discussion to bring about a successful conclusion to our initial ideas. Senior leadership of LEI, and UNCF President and CEO, Dr. Michael L. Lomax, became the driving forces of the LEI-UNCF partnership which enabled ideas to become more concrete. Dr. Brian Bridges, UNCF's Vice President for Research and Member Engagement, was in charge of the Institute for Capacity Building, and Angela Van Croft, UNCF's Director of Foundation and Corporate Relations, authored the proposal submitted to LEI. Dr. Lomax and I were part of the formation leadership team. My role, as in years past, was that of primary relationship manager to LEI for the UNCF development team. In that capacity, more than $1.5 million was granted to reinforce UNCF's ability to help students attending HBCUs and predominantly Black institutions (PBI) better prepare for careers and transition into meaningful jobs immediately upon graduation.

Under the proposal UNCF submitted, Dr. Bridges was to lead the Career Pathways Initiative, if funded by LEI. At the time, Ms. Van Croft described the goal as "to assist colleges and universities with the task of helping students find jobs in their particular area of expertise. It could be STEM, or it could be another area. The initiative will also serve to help schools beef up their career services centers."

LEI funded the UNCF proposal with a generous grant of $50 million, tied for the second largest grant in UNCF history. Primary focus for funding was UNCF's Career Pathways Initiative, to help address the unemployment and underemployment crisis among recent college graduates, and to aid HBCU and PBI students gain the knowledge, preparation, insight and skills needed for meaningful employment in a constantly evolving global economy.

In an October 2015 press release, an enthusiastic Dr. Lomax stated, "We have designed a program that we envision will serve as a model of best practices to solve the unemployment and underemployment crisis among recent college graduates...In today's marketplace, students need both the knowledge and soft skills to compete in a global economy. Sadly, too many of our nation's talented students are having difficulty finding good jobs after graduation. Our goal is to work with students, faculty, colleges, alumni, and employers to better connect the student experience with the jobs of the future."

In the same release, LEI's Chairman, President, and CEO, Clay Robbins, said, "The initiative will improve educational experiences for thousands of college students, and expand their ability to secure meaningful career opportunities." Eighty-seven public and private four-year HBCUs and PBIs across the United States were eligible to apply for competitive grants, as a result of LEI generosity. Twenty-four institutions were awarded implementation grants and will spend the next five years aligning curricula with workforce expectations, enhancing campus-employer partnerships, and providing faculty training opportunities, among other initiatives, to enhance students' career preparation.

When I received the good news concerning the LEI grant, all I could think about was this is an amazing program that is going to transform the lives of so many students. I was part of a comprehensive team that did something good and landed the second largest gift in UNCF history. I called my husband to share the good news. And, I still get goose bumps when I see a picture of that $50 million check.

To answer the phone and get the news that our program was funded at $50 million was not only life-changing for the benefitting students, but also for me as a resource development professional. Through my work at UNCF, I am leading the change that I want to see, having an impact on the lives of many and on the world.

Lessons Learned

There are both personal and professional lessons learned from such an adventurous experience.

First, I found out I am a fighter and I have great resilience. When the gift was announced on October 5, 2015, my faith and patience held me in good stead. I did not give up at any time over a period of four years. I saw that I was effective in building trust, relationships, and rapport with key players involved in this joint effort.

Second, it sounds like a cliché, but hard work does breed success. We were never able to take our foot off the gas pedal in four years, even though success seemed to come, all too often, in inches, instead of feet or yards. Success doesn't happen overnight. I discovered many bricks are needed to build a foundation for success.

Third, you need to be effective and relevant in the lives of those you seek to serve. One must be both high-touch and high-tech. In order to talk the talk, you must be able to walk the walk.

Finally, you win as a team and you lose as a team. I was fortunate to be part of a great team.

One Last Thought

Our daughter recently enrolled at Xavier University in New Orleans. There we were, in parent-student orientation, and can you believe what they talked about? Can you believe what they stressed? The Career Pathways Initiative. Living a lesson learned from my mother, Evelyn Ford: "Pay it forward by giving it back, no matter how small."

About Andrea Neely

Neely

For the past twelve years Indianapolis native Andrea Neely has provided stellar leadership in her role as Area Development Director, and for the past seven years, as the Indianapolis Regional Development Director for UNCF. Each year, using scholarships, internships and fellowships, UNCF helps more than 10,000 promising African American and other students of color attend college. Andrea manages office operations for Indiana and Ohio with annual campaigns of $2.5 million and other statewide initiatives. Since 2006, under her leadership $68 million has been raised to support the 37 UNCF colleges and universities and minority scholars who also attend Indiana state schools. The Indianapolis area office was recognized nationally by UNCF in 2017 as a top-performing office, having exceeded its annual campaign goal for the past four years. In 2016, the Indianapolis area office was the number one performing area office in the country, raising $26 million. Andrea was presented with the UNCF Award of Excellence for exceeding her annual fundraising goal 2014 to 2017.

Prior to joining UNCF, this accomplished fundraiser founded and led an economic development consulting firm for ten years. Her firm was praised by President Bush in his remarks during his attendance at Indiana Black Expo's corporate luncheon for its role in developing affordable housing for Indianapolis seniors through the local HUD office. Andrea was the first African-American female consultant from Indiana to submit a $4.1 million dollar HUD 202 application that was funded on its first submission.

Andrea has received numerous recognitions beyond UNCF: a "Breakthrough Woman" in education by the National Coalition of 100 Black Women, 2014; an Indiana Woman of Achievement by Ball State University for promoting educational opportunities statewide, 2011; the

Madam C.J. Walker Outstanding Woman of the Year Award for her community service and leadership, Center for Leadership Development, 2009; and the Partner In Progress Award for her statewide leadership in advancing education by Lieutenant Governor Becky Skillman. Andrea was appointed by Mayor Greg Ballard (2015) and Mayor Joe Hogsett (2017) to serve as a member of the Indianapolis Charter School Board, and was selected by Theresa Lubbers, Indiana Commissioner for Higher Education, to serve on the 21st Century Scholarship Advisory Council.

Andrea holds a Bachelor's degree in Public Affairs from Indiana University. She is a 2012 Hoosier Fellow alumna of the Indiana University Randall L. Tobias Center for Leadership Excellence. She is committed to advancing youth leadership development as a member and President of the Indianapolis Chapter of Jack and Jill of America, Inc.

Andrea is married to George Neely C.E.C., and the mother of four children: Paige, Lauren, and twins Blake and Julian.

CHAPTER FOUR

Planting Seeds

By Danny Dean

On November 4, 1992, when I started my position as President of the Indianapolis Public Library Foundation, I had already been in the fundraising profession for six years. Since 1986, I had served as Assistant Dean and Director of Development for the Indiana University (IU) School of Dentistry. I had been raising funds for the IU School of Dentistry and also worked on IU's Campaign for Indiana.

At the time, I worked with a dental school alumnus who was interested in making a gift of land to the dental school. The land was appraised for several million dollars—my first million-dollar gift! Well, not so fast. I left the dental school in 1992, and later learned that the donor had passed away and there had been little attempt to cultivate the spouse, so she decided to leave the land to another university. So, for me, still no million-dollar gift.

As with many of us who work for supporting fundraising organizations, it is important that we always maintain good communication with the leadership of the primary organization we serve. At the Library Foundation, I pledged to the CEO that I would always provide them with support and good communication. I also let them know that if they ever needed my assistance on any issue, I would welcome the opportunity to help, and, most importantly, I would do my best to make sure they were never surprised. I asked the same from them. During my time at the Library Foundation, I worked with six different CEOs, and, for the most part, the agreement worked well.

So I was not surprised when, in 1997, then Library CEO Ed Szynaka invited me to his office because he needed a favor. When I arrived, I noticed that Ed was more serious than usual. He asked me to have a seat and told me that he had an idea, and he hoped he could count on me for help. He told me it was his vision to renovate the downtown Central Library, which was housed in the Cret Building, built in 1917. It did not take much to convince me of the merit of his plan since both library staff and the public believed the building, named after Paul Cret, a French architect and designer of the building, was overdue for renovation. Having had only a partial remodel over the years, and with technology knocking on our doorstep, this idea was not only welcome but necessary. To this day, when I visit our Central Library, I think about Ed Szynaka and how his vision helped Indianapolis become home to one of the best public libraries in the country.

During our meeting, I asked Ed, "How can I help?" He told me it would cost approximately $105 million to build an addition and to renovate the Cret Building, and that from his discussions with members of the city council, they were not willing to spend that much money on the project. Ed believed if he could tell the city council that our Foundation would raise half of the money, they may be willing to support the renovation.

My response was, "So you want us to raise over $52 million?" Ed quickly said if the Foundation could raise $50 million, and if a few adjustments could be made to the project, $50 million would be sufficient.

Although the Library Foundation had shown growth over the last few years, raising on average a couple of million dollars a year was a far cry from $50 million. Additionally, the $2 million required for current library programs and operations also had to be raised. I told Ed I would talk with my Executive Committee and Board and get back with him. As I left Ed's office, I was flattered, but I was also in shock. It pleased me that Ed had enough confidence in our Foundation that he would come to us to help make this major project a reality. I wanted to fulfill my commitment to him and make this work.

My staff over the years will tell you that I like to use the phrase, "we need to be planting seeds." After I returned to my office, I realized that I needed to start "digging." So, on that day, I made my first phone call concerning the Central Library renovation.

Throughout the years, I had developed a nice relationship with Betty Roberts, who was the Administrative Assistant to Allen Clowes, a leading Indianapolis philanthropist. She had been helpful in the Library Foundation receiving funding from the Clowes Fund, a family foundation, for projects that would benefit library patrons and the Indianapolis community. Betty was nice, but tough, and very protective of Allen. When I phoned her that day, I told her that I wanted to give her important information about a future project for Indianapolis.

I asked Betty if I could meet with Allen. After a moment of silence, she told me he had not been out of his home for several months due to his health, and that it would be unlikely that she would be able to schedule a meeting. Just as I began to tell her I understood, she asked, "Can you go on a moment's notice?" Excitedly, I responded, "Of course!" She told me in the next few months she would call me if she could arrange a meeting with Allen and to be ready. Although I was optimistic, I was also realistic, and knew there was a possibility that the meeting may never happen. But, it was the start of "planting season" for me.

A few months later, Betty called. Looking back, I suspect it must be like when an actor receives a callback to audition for a desperately wanted role. In 48 hours, I had the opportunity to meet with the Director/Producer and secure my part. I was scheduled to meet with Allen at 3 p.m. for tea, at his home in Westerly, a well-established neighborhood near the Indianapolis Museum of Art. Being a guy from a small rural town in southern Indiana, I had never had afternoon tea; however, I looked forward to the experience, and to meeting Allen.

I made sure I was on time for my appointment. In fact, the day before my appointment, I drove to the neighborhood and located the house so there would be no chance for error. After ringing the doorbell, it was only a matter of moments until a young man dressed in a white coat invited me inside to join Allen. I was told we would be meeting in the library, and that he was there waiting for me. As we walked down the hall, I did a final check of my necktie and coat.

Allen was already seated on the sofa as I entered the room. Although he was unable to rise, he greeted me with a warm, welcoming smile, which immediately made me feel comfortable. The beautiful wood finishes in the room made the room a little dark; however, all of the books and suspected gifts provided a look of brightness. I took my seat across from Allen.

Over the years, I have talked with friends and colleagues about those moments when you are sharing space with well-recognized, accomplished, and famous individuals. In almost all cases, there was a plan or an action that led to that moment. In my career, something I have learned is that I am responsible for making things happen. Involving others in the process or getting assistance from others can be extremely helpful, but taking the lead in creating a million-dollar moment is what good fundraisers do.

After thanking him for meeting with me, I assured Allen I would be respectful of his time and not overstay my invitation. We then did what I call the "Hoosier Dance," exchanging pleasantries and small talk. After approximately twenty minutes, I began to talk about the library and how it benefits the citizens of Indianapolis, especially underserved populations. I mentioned the Central Library never had a major renovation, and discussed the role technology would be playing in our changing society. I stressed the necessity that the library be positioned to meet that need. I also pointed out that Central Library opened in 1917, the same year Allen was born. I was building the case for support.

The conversation was comfortable and pleasant. Allen was a charming host, and I could understand why he had the reputation of hosting dinner parties that guests enjoyed attending. After about an hour, I told him I probably should be going so as not to overstay my visit. Needless to say, I was pleased when he asked me to stay a bit longer as he was enjoying the conversation. Music to a fundraiser's ears!

During the next hour, we discussed various subjects related to the library and the city of Indianapolis. Allen had a special interest in how our public library branches had been strategically placed in the neighborhoods of Indianapolis. He then told me to call Betty the next day and schedule a second afternoon tea with him. He asked that I bring a map of the city of Indianapolis along with the location of all of the library branches.

As fundraisers, this kind of interest is what we hope for in a meeting with a prospect. I had been given an assignment, and, as I have learned, it is the manner in which we handle an assignment that may determine whether or not a gift is given and at what level.

It just so happened that Bob Kennedy, a well-known Indianapolis architect, was working at the library as the Associate Director of Facilities Management. I thought it would be helpful if Bob joined me on my next visit with Allen. Bob was willing to put together the map showing the library branch locations and attend the meeting with Allen. Of course, it was important to get approval from Betty and Allen for Bob to join us. Both were pleased to have Bob attend the meeting and share his expertise and experience. This is an example of one of those occasions when getting the right person to assist can be helpful in securing a major gift.

Bob and I arrived to meet with Allen, who again welcomed us warmly. For the next 90 minutes, we discussed the city of Indianapolis and the public library system. Allen asked numerous questions, and I believe Bob and I answered them well. I will always be grateful to Bob for helping me fulfill my assignment. As we drove away, we both felt fortunate to have been a part of what would become a significant and historical meeting with Allen Whitehill Clowes.

Unfortunately, that was my final visit with Allen. He passed away on November 1, 2000, at the age of 83. It would have been nice to have had more visits with Allen. Now, I could only appreciate my two meetings and be appreciative to Betty for allowing me to meet this special man.

I continued "planting seeds" and meeting with Ed Syznaka, the Library CEO, to follow the progress of the project. The city council had agreed with Ed's idea of a public and private partnership, so we were on our way. We hired a fundraising consultant and conducted a feasibility study following the approval of our Foundation Board and the establishment of a fundraising committee comprised of 25 city leaders.

Now that Allen had passed, was there still an opportunity for a gift for the Central Library renovation? I phoned Betty to ask her advice. That call provided me with some surprising news. Many assumed that once Allen passed away his estate would go to the Clowes Fund. However, she informed me Allen had decided to start a separate foundation with his estate known as The Allen Whitehill Clowes Charitable Foundation. The foundation's purpose, which would start with assets of $140 million, was to support the arts and humanities in Indiana.

I asked if the Library Foundation would be able to submit a request to the Clowes Foundation for the Central Library Project. She said Allen had shared his excitement about the project with her and that she would be happy to speak with Bill Marshall, the new president of the Clowes Foundation. In addition, she suggested I meet with her and Bill.

After scheduling my meeting with them, I began to work on our request. I have always been a fan of going to a solicitation meeting with a potential donor and providing a "menu." In other words, I like to present two or three ideas that may be interesting to a prospective donor. This way, if one of the ideas does not excite the prospective donor, perhaps, one of the alternate ideas will be more appealing. This strategy also decreases the chances of needing to start over. One cautionary note is that you must not appear to be wishy-washy. As a fundraiser, you must show commitment to each idea. You must be able to convey to the prospective donor that all of the ideas have value. Additionally, if the ideas have varying costs associated with them, the prospect has the opportunity to choose the idea that is more aligned with their gift expectation.

While meeting with Betty and Bill, I presented three ideas that would be naming opportunities in the new addition of Central Library. The ideas included naming opportunities for the Atrium at $4 million, the Auditorium at $2 million, and the Family Information Center at $5 million. I displayed the architect's plans for each space and indicated the number of people who would be expected, on an annual basis, to use each space. I explained how the spaces would be used for programs and special events, all touching many people's lives, especially those who are underserved. Throughout the meeting, it was apparent that Bill was a great supporter of libraries. At the conclusion of the meeting, they indicated they would take the information I had shared to the board of directors and contact me after the meeting. I followed up with a thank you letter and continued my "seed planting."

It is important to note a feasibility study was being conducted, and Betty was to be interviewed by our fundraising consultant. After the interview, the consultant came to my office to tell me we would not be receiving anything from the Clowes Foundation. I was shocked at his news and could not believe that my prior meetings would not produce a gift. My plan was to call Betty the following morning; however, before I could call her, she contacted me. She began the conversation by asking me about the man who had interviewed her the day before. Apparently she wasn't a fan, because, before I could respond, she said, "I did not like him!" I told her he was our consultant and that he was only doing his job, which was to assist the foundation with having a successful campaign. She appeared to be okay with my answer; nevertheless, she was clear that she did not want any more visitors. When I shared this information with our consultant, and told him that I remained hopeful that we would receive a gift, his response was, "I hope you are right and I am wrong."

After several weeks had passed, I received a phone call from Betty who asked me what time I would be home that evening. My response was, "When do you want me to be home?" We agreed on 6:30 p.m. Could this be my first million-dollar gift? It was difficult to know if this was going to be good news or bad news. Did she want to ask more questions? Was she going to give me bad news? I would just have to wait to find out, like fundraisers are trained to do.

At 6:30 p.m., I was waiting by the phone for her call. As the phone rang, I picked it up and hoped for the best. After exchanging our hellos, Betty said, "I am even going to surprise you." I didn't know what that meant, but it sounded encouraging. I responded, "I hope in a good way." She then said, "We have decided to do all three projects, totaling $11 million."

That was perhaps the best phone call I have ever received. Of course, I immediately expressed appreciation to her and the board for their generous gift. There was also a special moment that I thought about Allen and hoped he was witnessing the discussion.

I announced the gift the next day. It was on the front page of the

Indianapolis Star the following day. My first $1 million gift had turned into an $11 million gift. I realized that my professional life had changed.

The day after the gift was announced, our campaign consultant came to my office with a wrapped gift box. He presented it to me and asked that I open it. Inside was a glass piece was engraved with the words "Danny, Way to Go!" I appreciated his kindness and believed it was his way of saying, "I'm sure glad you were right and I was wrong" about the Clowes Foundation. Ever since, when a staff member receives a $1 million gift, I have given them a similar glass piece with a special message inscribed congratulating them on their success. It is my way of saying "welcome to the club."

My staff will tell you that another one of my favorite sayings is "Once the gift is made, that is when the work really starts." Well, the gift was for naming rights to three areas in a prominent building yet to be built in Indianapolis, so we had to make sure that all the details were correct.

I am so proud of the millions of lives those three areas in Central Library have since touched. I want to thank everyone and express appreciation to our campaign staff and volunteers for their hard work and devotion to detail during the building of Central Library. It is because of all of them that we were successful.

Post Script

In April 2004, I was invited to be a director of the Allen Whitehill Clowes Charitable Foundation Board. Today, I serve as the foundation's Chairman of the Board, which is one of the greatest honors of my life. Sometimes, we, as fundraisers, may never know how building relationships, a willingness to help others, and "planting seeds" can lead us to places we never suspected.

My best to all fundraising professionals. I hope your "seed planting" produces many million-dollar moments.

About Danny R. Dean

Dean

Danny Dean is the Major Gifts and Donor Liaison for the Indianapolis Public Library Foundation, after leading the Library Foundation as President since November 1992. As President of the Library Foundation, Danny led a successful Central Library Capital Campaign that raised $47 million. During his years as the Library Foundation President, the Foundation's assets increased from $1 million to more than $20 million, and annual revenues increased from $200,000 to more than $3 million.

Danny also serves as Chairman of the Board of the Allen Whitehill Clowes Charitable Foundation, a private foundation that provides support to charitable organizations that promote or preserve the arts and humanities, mostly in Central Indiana.

Prior to his position with the Library Foundation, he was Assistant Dean and Director of Development at the Indiana University School of Dentistry, and worked at the Indiana University Foundation on the Campaign for Indiana.

A graduate of Indiana State University, he serves on the Indiana State University President's National Advisory Committee, and is past-President of the Indiana State University Alumni Council. Danny also chaired the Board of the Indiana Council for the Advancement and Support of Education. He left his mark on the Indiana Council of Fundraising Executives Board, the Rotary Club of Indianapolis Board, the Finish Line Youth Foundation Board, the 500 Festival Board of Directors, and the 500 Festival Foundation Board. Additionally, Danny has mentored many fundraising professionals in Indiana and nationwide throughout his career.

His work positively impacted Marion County, Indiana adults, children, and families through programs funded within the Indianapolis

Public Library System such as the Summer Reading Program and The House That Readers Built, both of which have received national recognition. When Eugene Glick, an avid reader, community leader, and philanthropist, had an idea to honor Hoosier writers, Danny created the Eugene and Marilyn Glick Indiana Authors Award to celebrate and honor authors who have Hoosier roots or connections.

On the 20th anniversary of his presidency of the Indianapolis Library Foundation, in November, 2012, Danny was awarded the Governor's Distinguished Service Award and received proclamations from the City-County Council of Indianapolis, Indiana State University, and from the Office of the Mayor of Indianapolis in recognition of Danny's dedicated service to the citizens of Indianapolis and the state of Indiana.

Danny enjoys spending time with his wife, Debbie, attending movies, theater productions, baseball games, and Indianapolis 500 Festival activities and the Indianapolis 500.

CHAPTER FIVE
The Match and Roundup River Ranch, A SeriousFun Children's Network Story
By Ruth Johnson, JD, with Rick Markoff

Tom Schweizer and I have been friends since 1968, when we were fraternity brothers at the University of Missouri. Not long ago, Tom commented that he had volunteered at a camp in Colorado for seven years. This was not just any camp. It was Roundup River Ranch, a member of the SeriousFun Children's Network.

Roundup River Ranch began with a dream to carry out the vision of actor Paul Newman, and bring a Hole in the Wall Gang Camp (now SeriousFun Children's Network) to Colorado. The mission of SeriousFun Children's Network is to "create opportunities for children and their families to reach beyond serious illness and discover joy, confidence and a new world of possibilities, always free of charge."

When the first Hole in the Wall Gang Camp opened in 1988 in Ashford, Connecticut, it marked the realization of Newman's dream of starting "a free camp where kids could escape the fear and isolation of their medical conditions." There are now 30 camps around the world, nineteen of which are in the United States. Every year they continue to serve children diagnosed with severe medical conditions.

Two members of the Hole in the Wall Board of Directors, David Horvitz and John Forester, envisioned a camp set somewhere in the beautiful Rocky Mountains. In 2006, Alison Knapp, a local philanthropist, officially founded Roundup River Ranch. Alison later recalled, "I was fortunate enough to meet with Paul Newman before he died, and he seemed very pleased with what we had in mind."[1] She recruited a diverse founding Board of Directors and Ruth Johnson who became the camp's first and only President and CEO.

A native of Traverse City, Michigan, Ruth attended Albion College and the University of Michigan Law School. A 25-year business and legal career enabled Ruth to volunteer on a number of boards in the Vail Valley area. Alison developed an appreciation for Ruth's work and made a passionate appeal for Ruth to head the planned Roundup River Ranch. It was an appeal that Ruth could not refuse. Together, Alison and Ruth enlisted a dedicated group of staff, volunteers, community, and corporate partners. Together, they worked tirelessly to ensure Roundup River Ranch would be ready to open in July 2011.

One of Ruth's other motivations to join Alison was slightly more personal. She had friends in Denver whose child had been diagnosed with cancer. Ruth had always gladly given of herself to organizations that helped families, so deciding to help with Roundup River Ranch was instinctual. Her friends' child recently celebrated his 30th birthday.

Incredible time and effort went into the opening of Roundup River Ranch. It was five years in the making. The strategic plan for Roundup River Ranch called for $20 million in funding. Approximately one-third had been raised when Alison read an article in Forbes magazine about T. Denny Sanford, a South Dakota businessman and nationally-recognized philanthropist. At the time, he was in the Forbes listing of 500 richest people in the world with a net worth of $2.8 billion. Alison decided she would reach out to Denny once she found out he owned a home in the Vail Valley, and that he was extremely interested in helping children and children with medical issues.

Alison connected with Denny through a mutual friend. She sent him an e-mail about the vision and mission of the proposed children's camp, which was to be built in Dotsero, Colorado. Whatever Alison wrote must have struck a chord with Denny because he agreed to meet with both Alison and Ruth at his home in 2007.

Details of that meeting were still very vivid in Ruth's mind, 10 years later. "He was incredibly gracious and impressed with the proposed Roundup River Ranch (RRR). Denny wanted to hear about the RRR business plan, progress to date, what success looked like, and what next steps were." Ruth told him they needed to raise $20 million and they already had $6 million in pledges and gifts. She recalled Denny said, "I have a great feeling about this… I will create a match and leverage this for you. Raise $7 million dollars, and I will match it for you."

Everything happened very quickly. Ruth immediately returned to her office and wrote up the gift agreement. Ruth and Denny signed the agreement a short time later, but not without a surprise twist. Alison took the opportunity to display her prowess as master fundraiser. She asked Denny if he would consider doing a million-dollar gift up front in an effort encourage potential donors to meet the match. Denny agreed.

With the agreement in hand, Alison and Ruth introduced Denny to people who were involved with the project, both financially and significantly, balancing community leaders with staff and board leadership. Two of those board members were David Horvitz and John Forester, the duo who initially envisioned the camp. David and Denny's early meeting added creditability to the RRR effort, especially since David had already made a million dollar contribution to the campaign.

In the coming years, Ruth and Alison would experience what many nonprofit leaders experience during a major fundraising campaign. "The hours are long and the pay is not always competitive. You must respond to demands made upon you. Sacrifices are made to make the mission come alive," Ruth said.

The sacrifices, however, are offset by life experiences rarely found in other careers. For instance, Denny's energy was a perfect match with Alison's determination. His philanthropy allowed RRR to raise money during the economic downturn of 2008 and 2009 and helped it gain incredible momentum as staff and volunteers always thought goal was within reach. It also gave RRR leverage, as everyone knew Denny wanted the match to be successful.

Just like Denny, all of the donors were surprisingly approachable according to Ruth. "We had, and have, a lot to learn from Denny. We constantly sought his advice and guidance. We interviewed, and continue to interview, him as a mentor." Because of Denny, Ruth found other donors, board members, and staff had a lot in common with each other.

The matching gift campaign was a great success, and Roundup River Ranch opened in July 2011. Since it opened, the lives of thousands of campers and their families have been touched by RRR. Newman's vision of a place where kids can "raise a little hell" and have the chance to be fun-loving, worry-free kids had been realized, yet again. Roundup River Ranch served 1,400 children in 2017. Some 5,000 children with some of the most severe illnesses have enjoyed life-changing experiences, free of charge, since RRR opened.

Ruth learned a number of valuable lessons thanks to Denny's million-dollar moment: you need to talk to a lot of people; accept the idea that a lot of people will tell you to go for it, but they might not invest at that time—they may become advocates or donors at a later time; peers give to other peers; communication and gratitude never end; preserve the history of an organization; and, seek advice and good things will happen.

One of the many heartwarming stories about campers came in the early years of Roundup River Ranch.

"'In 2011, Cameron was diagnosed with leukemia,' said his father, Mike Hermes. 'He was only 6 1/2 years old when he started treatments. The next year, in 2012, we found out about Roundup River Ranch, and he was able to attend as one of the youngest campers there. Since then, he has gone five straight years in a row now, and he loves it.'"[2]

"Mr. Hermes continued, 'We had all these contingency plans in case something went wrong.' But much to his surprise, he said, 'We didn't hear from him for a week. We even went over a day early, and found him playing with new friends—he had absolutely no interest in going home early. After a really tough year, there was a marked change in Cameron. Camp was a tremendous opportunity for him to regain some confidence, and it helped our entire family, too.'"[3]

The ranch enjoyed Denny's continuing generosity. In 2014, with the intent to "help secure the organization's future," he pledged an additional $1 million to the ranch, which would be paid in $100,000 installments over the next ten years. "It's unbelievable to see the difference camp can make to these kids and families—camp is an oasis for them, and when they leave, they're stronger and happier. When I heard that a camper said his time at Roundup River Ranch was 'the best week of his life,' that it was the place he longed to be when he sat through hours of treatment and hospital stays, I knew that I needed to help," he remarked.

My college friend Tom recently asked if I would be a camp counselor with him at Roundup River Ranch next year so he wouldn't be the oldest guy there helping kids with severe heart conditions. I just might take him up on his request.

About Ruth B. Johnson, JD

Johnson

Ruth B. Johnson, JD, is President and CEO of Roundup River Ranch. RRR enriches the lives of children with serious illnesses and their families by offering free, medically-supported camp programs that provide unforgettable opportunities to discover joy, friendships, and confidence. Roundup River Ranch is a member of the SeriousFun Children's Network, the largest family of medical camps and programs in the world, which was founded by actor Paul Newman.

Ruth practiced law in the Denver, Colorado, area for more than 25 years prior to moving to the Vail Valley in 2005. She was an attorney for Amoco Corporation, General Counsel of ECOVA Corporation (an Amoco subsidiary), and an attorney with Davis Graham & Stubbs.

Her work as a real estate lawyer for Wear, Travers & Perkins law firm in Vail, Colorado, was a natural fit for her transition to help RRR with pro-bono legal work where she was instrumental in securing the initial formation and structure of the nonprofit with governmental approvals.

In July 2006, she was hired full-time by RRR and focused on securing the site, obtaining required governmental and judicial approvals for construction and orchestrating multiple resources from a team of architects, designers, developers, land planners, and staff.

Roundup River Ranch opened its camp in Dotsero, Colorado in 2011, and as of 2017 will have served 5,000 campers, all free of charge.

Ruth received her law degree from the University of Michigan, and has a bachelor's from Albion College with majors in economics and political science. At Albion, she was a member of the Professional Management Program. Ruth has been on the board of, and active in, many nonprofit, civic, and educational organizations in both Denver and the Vail Valley.

Ruth is married to Kris Sabel, Executive Director of the Vail Symposium. Residents of Avon, Colorado, they have two children, Kristen Kenly (34), and Brian Johnson (31). Kristen is married to James Kenly. They have two children and are living in the Vail Valley. Brian and his wife, Madeline Johnson, live in Victor, Idaho.

CHAPTER SIX
Phyllis and Walter, Friends Forever
By Dee Metaj

They had me at "hello."

Phyllis was petite, almost diminutive, hair perfectly coifed, manicured nails, beautifully dressed, articulate, bright as hell, and had a smile that would melt your heart. She was raised in Ontario, Canada.

Walter was tall, lumbering, somewhat socially awkward with a slight speech impediment, casual and easy-going. He had a sweet, bashful smile that belied his wicked sense of humor. He was raised by his father and grandmother on a chicken farm in Lansing, Michigan.

A mismatch if ever there was, and they adored each other. They were madly in love with their "four legged child" Mac, a white Westminster Terrier with the uncanny ability to look like he was smiling whenever he was happy.

When I received what would become a life-altering phone call in 1996, I was the first full-time director of development in the College of Osteopathic Medicine at Michigan State University (MSU). I began my development work at MSU in 1994 as the associate director of development for Corporate and Foundation Relations. This was the continuation of my work in Corporate and Foundation Relations at Olivet College in Olivet, Michigan, and as director of external relations at the Foundation for the Improvement of Education, the philanthropic arm of the National Education Association in Washington, D.C.

Dr. Timothy McKenna, a general surgeon and faculty member in the college, called to let me know he had given my name to his patient and her husband. The couple believed Dr. McKenna had saved her life, and so expressed their desire to do something for the college. This, of course, was almost a full decade before the Health Insurance Portability Accountability Act (HIPAA) went into effect in 2005.

As I was preparing to contact these new prospective donors, I was not quite sure about how best to handle the call. Dr. McKenna stated in the call that he had removed a small malignant tumor on her colon, and because they caught it so early, there was no need for any additional treatment. While this was certainly a great outcome, I didn't know these individuals and was really uncertain about the best approach given the possible sensitivities of the circumstances.

In preparation for the call, I developed my talking points with the strategy that I would take my lead from them based on how they responded. So here I was, all prepared for my very first grateful patient interaction (although I didn't understand it at the time), and got their answering machine. I quickly had to revise my plan to leave a message. I decided to leave a short, succinct, yet friendly message by letting them know I was following up on behalf of Dr. McKenna, and left my name and phone number and ended by saying that I was looking forward to talking with them. Walter returned my call the same day and asked if I would come to their home to talk about doing something for Dr. McKenna and the college.

It wasn't until I was lost en route that I realized the name of the street they lived on was the same as their last name. As I pulled up to their mid-1960s bungalow on the border of Lansing and Holt, Michigan, my initial reaction was this would likely be a modest gift based on the location and size of their home. What I missed was the significant expanse of land surrounding their home.

Walter filled the doorframe as he waited to greet me, grinning from ear to ear. So was Mac. Phyllis, dressed in a skirt, matching jacket, and very fashionable shoes, was at the kitchen table waiting with freshly brewed coffee and a variety of homemade pastries. We immediately settled into casual conversation at the kitchen table. It was clear that before we were going to get into a discussion about a gift they intended to make, they were going to get to know me better, and they were going to take stock of who was representing the college.

That first meeting lasted more than two hours. They wanted to know more about the college, of course, and they were extremely interested in me, both professionally and personally. I shared I was an MSU graduate, that I'd been at the university since 1994, and at the College of Osteopathic Medicine in a part- and full-time capacity since 1995; I was married with a 16-year-old daughter, two Golden Retrievers, two cats, and two hamsters that I desperately hoped were the same sex. While they were interested in the information about my professional life, what I believe was instrumental in gaining their confidence was my personal history. I think living in the nearby community, having a family and a number of pets made them feel I could relate to them.

In return, I learned a great deal about them. Phyllis was raised in Canada and became a naturalized citizen in 1942. Very shortly thereafter, she joined the US Navy as a WAVE and was discharged after the end of WWII. Walter and Phyllis married in 1959. Phyllis went to work for then Senator William Milliken, continuing as his personal secretary after he was elected Governor of the State of Michigan. Walter established the family farm as the Dell Centennial Farm in Holt, Michigan. He managed all aspects of the more than 26 acre farm located right behind their home, and in 1980 converted to a primarily soybean crop. He served in a number of community roles, but was most proud to be the statistician for the Detroit Lions football team for a number of years, well into his eighties.

About mid-way through our visit, Walter indicated he wanted to establish a scholarship, and intended to do so by using appreciated stock. By this time we had moved to the living room. As I glanced around, there was no evidence of any sort of wealth. The two cars in the driveway were both mid-range Buicks. Phyllis wore a simple diamond solitaire wedding ring, and Walter wore a Timex watch because "it could take a licking and keep on ticking." There was no valuable art that I could see. Still, I really liked them and was going to give them the best experience possible to help them achieve their goal to honor Dr. McKenna, and do the right thing by providing much needed support to medical students.

We talked through the three types of scholarships they could establish, and it became clear they were interested in endowing a scholarship. We spoke about what type of medical students they wished to support with their scholarship. Clearly, they had given this a great deal of thought and had agreed in advance of our meeting how they wanted to honor Dr. McKenna.

After an in-depth discussion and exchange of information, they were beginning to settle on the idea of awarding scholarship support to third- and fourth-year medical students who intended to become surgeons. I suggested to Walter and Phyllis that after I had the opportunity to talk with the College's Scholarship Committee and the Department of Surgery to share and review the criteria they wanted to use, I would provide them with a preliminary gift agreement for their review. I asked if they would like me to send the draft document, or, if they preferred, I could deliver it. They were very firm about scheduling a time for me to bring the draft to them so we could review it together.

They were thrilled when I responded by saying "Of course!" Phyllis, who'd had a pretty intense look on her face through most of the discussion, shared that their only previous experience with philanthropy was with the Humane Society, and they would be leaving 80 percent of their estate to them. I complimented them on making such a generous gift to a wonderful organization. She responded by saying, "If you keep up this kind of work, Walter and I will consider leaving some portion to the College of Osteopathic Medicine."

Within the next 30 days, the gift agreement was completed and signed. Walter transferred stock to MSU at just under $30,000. Walter and Phyllis were anxious to have the first recipient receive the award in the fall and decided to make an additional contribution to the spending side of the endowment account to be available for immediate use. As soon as the recipient was selected, I arranged a lunch that included Walter, Phyllis, the dean of the college, the medical student, and myself. I was surprised by how shocked Phyllis and Walter were at the thought of the dean taking time out of his schedule to have lunch with them and the student who had received the scholarship. In turn, I was taken aback at how humble these two generous human beings were.

Over the course of the next year, I stayed in close touch with Phyllis and Walter to check in and see how they and Mac were doing. I also took the opportunity to keep them up-to-date about the college, and more specifically, about the basic science research related to cancer that was being undertaken by the college. At that time, great strides had been made through the discovery of the cancer fighting drug, cisplatin, by Dr. Barnie Rosenberg, who was a PhD researcher at MSU.

Apparently, both Walter and Phyllis were reading the information I was sending because I received a call from Walter who, as he always did, informed me about the average rainfall the city of Lansing had received over the last month. As usual, we had a very brief back and forth about the weather and some discussion about how the Lions were doing if it were during the football season, or his thoughts about college basketball if it was March Madness. Once we got down to the real business of his call, Walter said he'd been reading about, and was very interested in, the genetics of cell mutations and would like to talk with a researcher about that. I was floored.

I said, "Walter, as usual, you have surprised me yet again. Why don't I take you and Phyllis to lunch at the Kellogg Center so we can talk in greater detail about what you want to learn?" We met over a lunch of beef tenderloin for both of us (Walter refused to eat chicken because he'd had his fill growing up on a chicken farm), fish for Phyllis, coffee for three, and a shared desert between Walter and me because Phyllis frowned upon Walter eating a whole piece of pie with whipped cream on top and vanilla ice cream on the side. In the years to come, we'd still split desert even when Phyllis wasn't with us.

As it turned out, Walter was considering using a pesticide developed by Monsanto on his soybean crop and had become extremely interested genetic modification in all of its forms. I'd done my homework before the meeting by talking with the then dean, Al Jacobs, about who would be the best researcher to introduce to Walter and Phyllis. I was really concerned about the ability of any researcher to provide that kind of information in a way that would be understandable for a lay person. At Dr. Jacobs' suggestion, I met with Justin McCormick, PhD, a basic science researcher who had been doing extensive genetic research in finding what caused normal human cell production to turn into tumor producing, malignant cells. While Justin agreed to the meet, I explained my concern about how he would communicate with Phyllis and Walter in a way that would educate them but not intimidate them. Justin nodded throughout our conversation and assured me he would be able to help accomplish the goal.

The introductions were stiff and slightly awkward. Walter was in a suit and tie, Phyllis was also in a suit, and neither could relax and get comfortable as Justin showed them around the research laboratory. Maybe it was all of the scientific equipment, the hazardous waste sites, and/or being completely out of their element, but this meeting was not working, and I was about ready to chalk it up as a mistake until Justin showed them the "immunodeficient" mice, which were mice that were bred to have no immune system. Suddenly, Walter's face lit up, he started nodding his head with understanding, paused for a moment, and began to ask a slew of questions about what methods the scientist used to accomplish this, why was it important, and how did it apply to human beings. Walter cast a look in my direction, and with a confident smile, informed me he'd done some reading about this kind of research. I glanced over at Phyllis who laughed at her beloved husband and gave me a positively radiant smile. She leaned into me and whispered somewhat mischievously, "We may own a farm, and we may live on that farm, but we're far more than farmers, my dear."

Sitting at the round table in Justin's office over coffee and tea, he explained his research by simply using his hands to describe cancer cells and how he believed that cancer was caused by a normal cell that flips to become a malignant producing cell reproducing as only cancer cells that ultimately form tumors. He went on to explain that his research was focused on identifying which single human cell flips to become cancer-causing. Justin had magically created a meaningful opportunity to both inform and engage Walter and Phyllis in an entirely different manner by simply telling the story of how human cells grow and change, and his work to treat and ultimately cure cancer.

Rather than ask for any immediate feedback from their time with Justin, I let them have several weeks to digest and reflect on what they learned. Meanwhile, Justin sent a thank you note and offered to answer any questions they might have, and if they wished, he would be more than happy to meet with them. Walter circled back to me—because he didn't want to bother Justin—to ask about the students who were working in the lab the day Justin gave them the tour. I explained these were DO-PhD students who were in the Physician Scientist

Training Program—an elite group of students who would complete a combined degree as a Doctor of Osteopathy and a PhD in basic science simultaneously. Walter and Phyllis wanted to meet some of the students in the program.

The team decided to include Dr. Veronica Maher, a distinguished faculty researcher who had been working alongside Justin, in the next meeting with Phyllis and Walter since she had been primarily supervising these students. We hand-selected four students in the program who were to meet and share their experiences with Walter and Phyllis. All of the selected students were in their late twenties and early thirties. Three were married, and two of the three had at least one child. One of the women we selected had a husband who was also in the program, so we thought of this as the twofer (two-for-one) bonus strategy. While all of the students in the Physician Scientist Training Program had debt loads that would easily exceed $125,000, this couple would owe more than $250,000 by the time they graduated from the program.

The meeting was amazing and proved to be eye opening because the students were so remarkable. They were scary smart, funny, dedicated, and oh-so-down-to-earth. Yet, what was really moving: none had come from any sort of means. All had worked to pay for their undergraduate education with limited help from their parents. In one case, there was a first-generation student who had grown up on a farm. In all cases, they were hard working and tenacious. Walter and Phyllis were totally blown away.

The day they signed the gift agreement to establish the endowment to fund the DO-PhD Physician Scientist Training Program at MSU was one of the happiest of their lives. The path to that decision was not so easy, however. They struggled for several months, vacillating between endowing a cancer research fund or supporting the students who would be researchers and clinicians. While they realized the value of research and understood the crucial role it played in treatment and finding a cure, the idea of supporting basic science research was simply too amorphous. Instead, they determined they wanted to support the physician-scientists who would be spearheading the research to find better treatment modalities and maybe, one day, a cure.

The funding for the program was accomplished through a seven-figure gift, and made in honor of one another. The signing ceremony included freshly brewed coffee and homemade pastries. Walter wore a new suit and snazzy tie. As always, Phillis was impeccably dressed, and was wearing a very cool pair of gray Mary Jane heels.

Although I left the College of Osteopathic Medicine in late 1999 to become a planned giving officer at MSU, I continued to be Walter and Phyllis' primary development officer for the next six years. The college did a wonderful job of making sure Walter and Phyllis were introduced to and attended a luncheon with the students who were the recipients of their first scholarship, as well as keeping them engaged with the students in the DO-PhD Physician Scientist Training Program.

Shortly before I left MSU in 2005 to take a position at the Oregon Health and Sciences Foundation in Portland, Oregon, Walter, Phyllis and I went to dinner at the Kellogg Center at MSU. Over dinner, we decided that we would continue to stay in touch no matter where they were living or where I was working. We did, until Walter and Phyllis transitioned into a nursing home in 2009.

As I reflect on my various experiences over the number of years working with Phyllis and Walter to help them actualize their philanthropic passion—just as they have helped and will continue to support so many students achieve their dreams—I've come to understand that for me, theirs was a gift that keeps on giving.

If hindsight is 20-20, the two most obvious and immediate lessons I learned early in my career were: first, coming to the realization about the existence of the millionaire next door (before the book was published), how they think and behave; and second, the emergence of the "grateful patient" donor, and the significant impact they would have on the future of medical and hospital fundraising.

Over the more than twenty years since having the joy of working with Phyllis and Walter, their gifts to me, and the true pearls of wisdom I want to share, are centered on the understanding that developing a partnership with your donors to truly understand what they are passionate about, and how you, as their philanthropic advisor, can help them find and work to develop that opportunity, is ultimately your responsibility. What this really means and what it requires is the ability to check your ego, needs, and wants at the door, and genuinely work to understand what they wish to accomplish by asking questions—lots of questions—to get at the heart of their passion, and to help them achieve that goal. Listening in all of its forms is key to understanding the needs and wants of your donor. Developing trust in the relationship is vital. Trust your donors to know what they want to achieve, and, in turn, work to secure their trust by demonstrating at every turn that you are their philanthropic champion. Above all, treasure and care about them as human beings who want to leave this place better than they found it.

About Dorothy "Dee" Metaj

Metaj

Dee Metaj is a 25-year veteran of higher education fundraising. In her current role as Indiana University Foundation Vice President for Development, Indianapolis, she led the Indiana University-Purdue University Indianapolis IMPACT Campaign—the largest and most successful comprehensive fundraising campaign in the university's nearly 200-year history—which raised $1.39 billion, exceeding its initial goal of $1.25 billion.

A graduate of Michigan State University, she earned her Bachelor of Arts degree in the College of Social Science with a dual major in psychology and sociology. Shortly after graduation, she began her eight-year career in mental health by working with emotionally impaired adolescents in a state of Michigan residential treatment facility.

Her career path took an undecided yet very auspicious turn when she was asked by a former colleague to consider taking on the role of director of development and external relations at the National

Foundation for the Improvement of Education, the philanthropic arm of the National Education Association in Washington, D.C. While she loved working with children, she realized fundraising was what she was absolutely meant to do.

Her higher education fundraising experience began at Olivet College in Olivet, Michigan, where she established the college's first Corporate and Foundation Relations program. She then worked at Michigan State University for eleven years, serving as a senior development director and university planned giving officer, lead development officer in the College of Osteopathic Medicine, and associate director of Corporate and Foundation Relations.

Prior to returning to the Midwest and the Indiana University Foundation, she was the vice president of development at the Oregon Health and Sciences University Foundation in Portland, Oregon. She is a faculty member in The Fundraising School in the Lilly Family School of Philanthropy and a member of the AFP and CASE.

She lives in Indianapolis and is the proud mother of a daughter and son-in-law, and a grandmother to their beautiful daughter.

CHAPTER SEVEN
Meeting a Societal Need, Boys Town, USA
By Dennis Stefanacci

Project: Establishing the first Boys Town campus outside of Boys Town, Nebraska. Established in 1917, Boys Town (Father Flanagan's Boys Home) provides a safe refuge for troubled youth from across the country who have experienced the trials and tribulations of a tumultuous existence, and who, with the help of the Boys Town program, have ultimately found their way to a better future. The campus in Boys Town, Nebraska, is very large, and functions as its own town.

I was recruited to Boys Town in the mid-1980s to oversee and help expand their fundraising program. Until coming to Boys Town, I had served in resource development capacities at several colleges and universities, including the Catholic University of America in Washington, D.C. The organization was already raising millions of dollars annually through its direct mail and comprehensive planned gifts programs, and had been the beneficiary of a significant number of extraordinary legacy gifts over time. As one might expect, because of Boys Town's ability to communicate its story in a way that almost everyone could identify with, these estate gifts came from people of all ages and all walks of life from across the country, and are certainly a tribute to work being done daily by the Boys Town staff.

My role was to help the organization take the next step forward, while better communicating Boys Town's message to those committed to helping.

Our charge was to build on the program already established by reaching out to long-time significant supporters of Boys Town by developing personal relationships with them when possible.

We also expanded our efforts in the area of planned gifts by adding staff in that area with the intent to increase the already established program of visiting with those donors who previously made a gift of $100 or more to Boys Town, to both express our thanks and to make them "Honorary Boys" of Boys Town. Suffice it to say that once that relationship had been established, there was not only more of an opportunity to discuss a Charitable Gift Annuity with them, but also other life-income gifts, as well.

As we devoted more time and energy to these initiatives, it became clear that in order to take the next step in this process—to establish a significant major gifts program—we needed to spend more time in those communities where the need for Boys Town's services and programs was the greatest. As a result, we aimed to develop a better understanding of the ever-increasing need for Boys Town's offerings, not only nationally but also in those communities with the greatest need, and to seek financial support for the implementation of those efforts, both at the main campus and in those communities.

It was this exploration that led to a much more comprehensive development program that extended its reach far beyond anything it had done to date, and helped position the organization, from a fundraising perspective, for the idea of Boys Town USA.

While Boys Town had already served tens of thousands of children over its 70 year history at that time, it still was limited in the number of children it could reach by the mere size of the campus and the cottages that existed there. It just wasn't large enough to even begin to address the needs of those children who were abused and/or neglected throughout their young lives.

Father Robert Hupp, Executive Director of Boys Town at that time, realized this and decided that while Boys Town was addressing a significant societal need, both on the campus and through its exported parent-teacher program in facilities across the country, it just wasn't enough. The answer for him was simple: Boys Town USA, a concept establishing small campuses of three to five homes outside of Boys Town, Nebraska, that provided the same family experience as at the Nebraska campus for children in need, but in their own communities.

The first step was to explore those states where a significant number of children were being referred to Boys Town, and then to strategically think through the concept of Boys Town USA and how to best develop a "mini" campus, if you will, that would function as if these cottages were at the main campus.

Issues, of course, that needed to be explored included: How large would the campus be? How will the project be funded? Once online, how would its operations be funded annually? Would there be a need for a local Board? How would the community accept such group homes? Where would these children attend school?

These and other questions were explored at length at the main campus prior to the first state being selected. It also became clear in these discussions that it was very important that the capital dollars be raised from the community to ensure their ownership of the project, and that that community, with support from the main campus, assume responsibility for the financial support needed to operate the campus annually.

It was that vision and Boys Town's strategic plan for the implementation of these campuses that took us—Father Hupp and members of the development staff—to Oviedo, Florida. At that time, Florida had one of the highest referral rates to Boys Town's main campus. Further research took us to Oviedo as a small town that was not only rural in nature—yet not very far from urban Winter Park— but that also had a great school system with what appeared to be a group of dedicated community leaders whose reach extended beyond the Oviedo area.

Our approach was to first engage this group of community leaders in how we'd like to proceed, and once we had their support and approval, to initiate a series of meetings that they would host, not only for other members of the Oviedo community but for the surrounding communities, too. As it turned out, and as one might expect, we identified two major issues of concern: Would building such a campus for at-risk youth in their communities make their communities less safe? Would having such a campus in their area negatively impact property values?

These questions required a special person with a special message. Father Hupp was clearly the chosen one. This 70-year-old man—a true reflection of the human spirit and the good work that was being done by Boys Town—was not only able to address these issues head on in a very compassionate and articulate way but also establish an ongoing dialogue with the community that integrated them into the decision-making process. Subsequently, the community embraced this endeavor, providing the impetus we needed to raise the funds to underwrite the cost of developing the campus, a multi-million-dollar effort that to this day continues to be the founding principle behind the Boys Town USA program and the largest Boys Town USA campus in the United States.

Not surprisingly, Father Hupp's message was so convincing that several major donors stepped forward and agreed to lead this effort. The initial gifts, made by two members of the volunteer committee established to spearhead and oversee this effort—valued at more than $1 million—came in the form of the land on which the first three homes were built, and from a local family who directed their gift toward the construction of the campus. Both donors, who had an unwavering commitment to the well-being of children, and their willingness to lead by example, set the tone for the successful completion of this effort in a relatively short period of time.

The family that donated the land had large agricultural holdings just outside of Oviedo, which made the land they offered the ideal place to establish the campus. This location was far enough from town not to negatively affect land values or concern citizens that these children might be a threat, and close enough to provide residents of the campus with access to the school system and to businesses there.

The other major donor, who had a very large family and was highly respected in the Winter Park area, understood the importance of providing children such as these with every opportunity to lead a life better than the one in which they had been born. One could not be more privileged to work with such a family and to experience, first hand, their compassion and willingness to make a difference. While this family had significant wealth, their commitment was certainly a sacrificial gift. To this day, it is rare that I meet others like this family, although I have raised many million-dollar gifts over the years. They are special people, individuals who will always have a special place in my heart, because of their compassion for those less fortunate and truly in need.

Certainly the message here is clear: philanthropy is the art of matching organizational needs with donor interests. It's the engine that drives the interests and the fortunes of not-for-profit organizations to the next level, positioning them to achieve their goals and mission. Add to this a dedication to identifying and implementing a process that defines all the needs and issues of the organization or project, and then develops a plan to work within that process to achieve success.

This was the philosophy that was the basis of establishing the first Boys Town USA campus in Central Florida, realizing the needs and obstacles of taking such a step for the organization, and developing goals and objectives premised on the concept of strategic philanthropy. The result, of course, was the development of a plan that articulated the interim steps required to ensure success, and the ultimate implementation of that plan. From vision to completion and celebration, the Boys Town USA campus in Central Florida was affirmation that if one takes the time to develop the processes needed to garner success, and then exerts patience and perseveres, virtually any goal can be achieved.

Today, the programs and services of Boys Town USA Central Florida touch the lives of 7,600 children and families in Central Florida each year. Boys Town Central Florida has been recognized for its long history of serving as an excellent steward of its donor support. Charity Navigator, one of the nation's largest and most-respected charity rating systems, has awarded Boys Town its highest rating for sound management of finances. It is well-positioned to continue to save children and heal families throughout Central Florida.

About Dennis Stefanacci, ACRFE

Dennis Stefanacci is the founder and principal in the firm of Dennis Stefanacci & Associates, a consulting firm providing services in the area of external relations, with special emphasis in the development and implementation of strategic and comprehensive development and communications plans, board development, capital campaigns, and major and planned gift programs.

Stefanacci

Prior to starting his company in August 2002, Dennis was senior vice president for Corporate Social Responsibility at Starbucks Coffee Company in Seattle, Washington, with worldwide oversight of the company's business practices, environmental and community relations programs, corporate giving, and the Starbucks Foundation. He recently completed a five-year assignment as President & CEO of the Broward Health Foundation and Senior Vice President of Broward Health, where the Foundation experienced exponential growth, including the successful completion of an eighteen-month capital campaign for the renovation and expansion of the Salah Foundation Children's Hospital at Broward Health, exceeding the $20.6 million goal by more the $2 million.

Additionally, Dennis has served as Vice President of the Max Planck Florida Foundation in Jupiter, Florida, President and CEO of the Mt. Sinai Health Systems Foundation and Vice President of the Miami Beach based System; Senior Vice President of Institutional Advancement at Intracoastal Health Systems in Palm Beach County, Florida; and President and CEO of the Grant-Riverside Hospitals Foundation in Columbus, Ohio. He has held senior positions at the Toledo Museum of Art, Father Flanagan's Boys' Home (Boys Town), and at several colleges and universities, including the Catholic University of America in Washington, D.C.

Dennis has bachelor's and master's degrees in Sociology from the University of Pittsburgh in Pittsburgh, Pennsylvania, and is currently a PhD candidate in Political and Applied Sociology there. He has achieved the prestigious designation of Advanced Certified Fundraising Executive (ACFRE). He also earned professional and educational recognition from organizations such as the Association of Fundraising Professionals (AFP), which named him National Outstanding Fundraising Executive of the Year in 1996 and in 2015 named him Outstanding Fundraising Executive of the Year by the Ft. Lauderdale Chapter of AFP.

In 2017 Dennis was honored with the Lifetime Achievement Award from 2-1-1 Broward. Dennis has been active as a presenter both nationally and internationally on many topics and is also a dedicated community volunteer, having served on many volunteer boards throughout his career.

CHAPTER EIGHT
It Happened On 9/11
Dr. John S. Lore

Connectmichigan Alliance (CMA) grew out of an emerging concern among Michigan's nonprofit leaders that without a robust network of volunteers and an infrastructure for managing it, the sector would struggle. Many key leaders realized that this type of network's success would be greatly dependent on consistent public and private funding, both of which were uncertain and challenging.

The State of Michigan had long championed volunteerism and national service initiatives with its creation of the Michigan Community Service Commission (MCSC). In response, a campaign was started to create a permanent endowment to support and promote a coordinated volunteer program throughout all of Michigan

The collaborating organizations were the Michigan Community Service Commission (MCSC), Michigan Nonprofit Association (MNA), Michigan Campus Compact (MCC), and Volunteer Centers of Michigan (VCM).

The CMA Campaign began in earnest when the State approved the creation of a $10 million one-for-one challenge grant that would match funding from the nonprofit sector (i.e., corporate, private, family, and community foundations), the for-profit sector (i.e., corporations and sole proprietorships), and individuals. It was decided that a separate infrastructure organization should exist with a focus on volunteerism, and so CMA was formed in 2001.

I was appointed founding President and CEO, after retiring from the Ascension Health System in late 2000. My major responsibility was to lead the fundraising campaign and facilitate the efforts to raise a $20 million endowment to ensure the future of ConnectMichigan Alliance and volunteerism in Michigan.

My million-dollar moment occurred on September 11, 2001, while meeting with the Herbert H. and Grace A. Dow Foundation (HGDF) in Midland, Michigan. While preparing for this meeting, we knew this would be one of the most difficult funding requests we would have to make for several reasons: the $1 million level was stretching HGDF historical gift level for this type of program; historically, HGDF did not generally support our type of program beyond clearly identified regional boundaries; and HGDF was not at the same asset level as other large Michigan foundations such as W.K. Kellogg, Kresge, and C.S. Mott, which all contributed at the $1 million level.

Considering these challenges, along with a slowing economy, we knew this call would be challenging at best.

Our appointment was scheduled for 9 a.m. Eastern Standard Time, on September 11, 2001. Kyle Caldwell, President of MCSC, and Sam Singh, President of MNA, were driving together from Lansing, Michigan, while I was coming from Bay City, Michigan, only fifteen miles from Midland. I arrived to the HGDF Offices early and was going over our request documents when Kyle and Sam arrived and asked me if I had heard about the World Trade Center airplane crash. At that point Margaret Ann Riecker, President of HGDF, came out of the Board Room and asked us to stay until they decided what the Members of the Board would do.

Several of the Board Members were from New York, and one had a family member with offices in the World Trade Center. I immediately offered to reschedule our meeting and presentation. Margaret said "if timing and schedule are not an issue, I would really like the three of you to stay until we determine our course of action." We could hear the receptionist contacting other groups to cancel that day's scheduled calls and thought we would probably not be able to make our request that day.

About twenty minutes later, Margaret came out to the reception area and invited us to come into the room and make our request. With the incredible course of tragic events unfolding, we were absolutely amazed at the focus of the entire HGDF Board. Because most of the day's other meetings were canceled, we stayed for over two hours, answering a myriad of questions about CMA, volunteerism, and the endowment.

In our post strategy discussion after the presentation, we were not at all clear what the decision would be, or for that matter, when the decision would be made with the terrible and frightening events of the day. It would be safe to say that all three of us felt that our chances for rejection were much higher than a positive decision for all of the challenges mentioned and the awful events of the day.

Late that evening, I received a call from Margaret with the great news that our request had been granted at the full amount of $1 million. When I expressed my surprise because of the terrible events of that day, she said it was probably because of that tragedy they stretched their normal funding guidelines to make our award.

She indicated that generally after a Board Meeting the Board Members fly immediately back to their destinations. However, since all flights were cancelled the Board Members stayed for the full day and discussed our request, coming to the conclusion that "now is the time we need a coordinated volunteer effort in our nation."

While we will never know if our request would have been granted at any level, let alone the $1 million level, I am convinced that the importance of volunteerism was ever present in the minds of each and every HGDF Board Member on September 11. On a personal level, this gift made clear to me the belief of enlightened philanthropic foundations in the importance and value of volunteers resolving national, as well as local and regional problems.

The gift from HGDF encouraged other similar-sized foundations to stretch their funding levels and ensured the success of the $20 million endowment. As a result of the successful endowment, the MNA and MCSC moved their programs and endowments to support the new organization. CMA's commitment to building partnerships was demonstrated throughout the duration of its existence. CMA often worked to connect organizations with similar goals to facilitate learning communities and strengthen services provided, and help prevent the duplication of volunteer services both within communities and statewide. By cultivating state-level and local-level contacts, CMA was able to more effectively offer support to communities.

Even beyond these central resources and partnerships, CMA acted as a resource for the nonprofit sector through advocacy and educational initiatives. It provided opportunities for adults and students to engage with government through dialogues and programs, meetings with their state legislators, advocacy days, and the first student-community action network in the country. Today, the ConnectMichigan Alliance Endowment continues to fund programs and initiatives that advance volunteerism in Michigan as a part of the Michigan Nonprofit Association. The accomplishments have been measurable and valuable to Michigan.

There were several lessons learned from the HGDF gift on September 11, 2001. Chief among those was that with a compelling case need statement and presentation, informed grant makers can, and will, look beyond traditional decision making guidelines to invest a foundation's resources. An equally important lesson is that the events of the day can, and will, influence the grant- making considerations of enlightened grant makers. Clearly, the HGDF Board Members were an enlightened and thoughtful group on September 11, 2001.

My million-dollar moment will forever become a memorable and important part of the ConnectMichigan Alliance historical record.

About Dr. John S. Lore

Dr. John Lore served as a foundation intern to the CEO of the internationally recognized W.K. Kellogg Foundation. He led the development of the largest nonprofit hospital system in the world, Ascension Health. John served as chair of his national professional organization, the Association of Fundraising Professionals, and led a statewide public-private fundraising effort securing $20 million of endowment gifts to support volunteering in Michigan. He is one of Michigan's most honored leaders, having served as President/CEO of ConnectMichigan Alliance; President/CEO of SSJHS/Ascension Health; President of the Michigan Colleges Foundation (now called the Michigan Colleges Alliance); Chair of the National Society of Fundraising Professionals, 1993-94; and President of Nazareth College, 1972 to 1980.

Lore

After graduation from Western Michigan University, John began his career as a Management Trainee for Ford Motor Company. He returned to his alma mater as Director of Alumni and Development. While earning two more degrees from Western, John served as President of Nazareth College in Kalamazoo from 1972-80. His success at Nazareth was a key reason he was selected as President of the Michigan Colleges Foundation (renamed the Michigan Colleges Alliance). Seven years later, John was named President and CEO, Executive Vice President, of the Sisters of St. Joseph Health System and Ascension Health. His healthcare responsibilities ran from 1986 through 2000. John returned to the healthcare scene as consultant for Detroit Medical Center, 2005 to 2007.

His highly valued leadership and experience throughout Michigan made John a natural for the position of President and CEO of ConnectMichigan Alliance, and later, President and CEO of the Great Lakes Bay Regional Alliance.

John is proud of his time spent as Board Chair and Finance Committee Chair of the Marian Health System and Franciscan Health System in Tulsa, Oklahoma, and Baton Rouge, Louisiana.

Judy and John Lore now reside in Scottsdale, Arizona. They have two adult sons, Christopher and Matt, and two grandchildren.

CHAPTER NINE
Who? How Fast? For What?
By Frank Habib

"It was a dark and cloudy night, the wind howling, the lights went out, a shot was fired, a woman screamed." My path to a career in Development/Fundraising was nowhere near as dramatic. In fact it was more serendipitous.

Byron Tweeten, a professional colleague, long-time family friend and business partner, encouraged me to "throw my hat in the ring" for a Director of Development position at one of his clients—St. John's Military Academy (SJMA). I had declined twice before, but this time I consented to pursue the opportunity. I got the job and spent four-and-a-half years at the Academy.

I joined Byron's firm, Growth Design Corporation (GDC), Milwaukee, WI, as a consultant, and over the next eleven years, moved up to the position of Managing Consultant. During my time at GDC, I was involved with clients from Los Angeles to Atlanta.

I returned to SJMA for one-and-a-half years to do a turnaround of the Development Office: hire and train staff, establish systems, and create a national fundraising effort for annual and capital needs.

The Milwaukee School of Engineering (MSOE) was in a national search for a Vice President of Development, of which I knew nothing about. One day, while at SJMA, I received a call from Professor Ray Palmer, chair of their search committee, asking if I would stand for nomination for the position. My reaction was, "probably, if I knew what that meant." Through our continuing conversations and interviews, I was informed that I was nominated by an anonymous colleague. I spent the next eighteen years at MSOE as Vice President of Development.

This brings us to a critical juncture in the story. MSOE was undertaking its first major resource development program in more than a decade. The following narrative happened about two years into the campaign.

"We need a large major gift to sustain our momentum, and add to the excitement of our fundraising program." This is a common statement heard from virtually every President, board member, or Chief Development Officer in the throes of a major fundraising effort, campaign, or resource development program. The program is going well, early lead gifts are in, major donors are being cultivated, new major gift prospects are being identified and researched, however, there is always the "lull" somewhere in the middle of the effort. We were no different. Early major gifts had been secured. Several more were in process. This was our first major fundraising program in over a decade. Given all of the activity that was happening, we needed a big close. As added pressure, we would celebrate our Centennial Anniversary during the program.

A $1 million gift was just the ticket. But who? How fast? For what?

MSOE launched a major fundraising program between 1999 and 2004 to benefit the students and faculty. Our goal was to raise $48 million over a five-year period.

This was a significant challenge for the university, as the goal was more than twice the previous fundraising effort. A national consulting firm, in their feasibility study, had recommended that we could raise between $36 million and $40 million.

This vignette embodies three theoretical bases in fundraising: relationship management, the "fair exchange model," and, corporate-university partnership based on the interests and needs of both parties.

The university had an engineering alumnus who was president of a key division of a multi-national company. The alumnus was also a member of the Board of Regents. He and I had developed a very good professional and personal relationship. As a personal donor and our advocate at the corporation and their foundation, he was very interested in how they might support the major fundraising program that was being conducted. During the fundraising initiative, the university launched a bachelor's degree program in software engineering, the first of its type in Wisconsin at a private, non-research, and non-PhD granting university. The alumnus' company and division needed and wanted these graduates in their software research and development areas.

What became very clear is that the university, as a part of the fundraising initiative, had earmarked several million dollars in new program and laboratory development. A software engineering laboratory was definitely "in the mix." The university already had another named laboratory from the company on campus; the Division President and I worked to build on the existing, long-standing relationship. After considerable conversations with MSOE's President, campaign co-chairs, software engineering faculty, and the regent/ alumnus regarding the need, it was decided that the Vice President of Development would write a brief summary proposal that the alumnus/ regent would review with the Chairman of the company.

Interestingly enough, a longer, more elaborate proposal was discussed. The alumnus/regent suggested that the one or two page summary proposal would be enough to gauge the interest and inclination of the Chairman to fund the project. A perfect "trial ask" was the ticket. The proposal was developed, reviewed, revised, and approved by the university president, reviewed and revised by the Division's President, and personally reviewed with the Chairman of the company.

The crux of the proposal was that similar to the other named laboratory, the university would, for a $1 million gift, name the software engineering laboratory for the company, provide significant and highly visible signage, and build a conference room where their company engineers, university software engineering faculty, and students could work together on any number of "front and back burner" projects for, and on behalf of, the company.

He reviewed the proposal with the Chairman, and one week later informed me it was approved, and the funding model was agreed upon. Half of the funds would come from the company division and half from their foundation. The alumnus/regent and the president of the university were absolutely ecstatic with the results. The laboratory was built and served as a "jump start" to several other pending major gifts.

The project is a testament to developing a personal/professional relationship management process, exemplifies the very essence of "fair exchange," and sustains a long-term corporate/university partnership.

A definite win, win, win. This gift was newsworthy and provided "the lift" we needed at the time. The fundraising program, "Second Century Challenge," was a great success, and we raised $77 million.

Here are the lessons learned from my million dollar moment: We are not a transaction business, but rather a transformational business. The essence of our profession is "relationship management." The "fair exchange" model is often overlooked when working with business—they are run by people who have needs and wants, as well. Too often, we think "more is more;" rather in this instance, by listening to our key leaders and major gift prospects, we can learn that "less is more." Finally, critical to success is involving key leadership to deepen their commitment to the organization.

About Frank Habib

Habib

Frank Habib, President, Frank Habib and Associates, LLC, has over 36 years in the development field, all at the senior management level. His expertise is reflected in his broad-based experience in health care, education, and social services. He is skilled in fundraising strategy, major donor development, program design, staff development, and mentoring.

As the consultant to Regional Health and the Regional Health Foundation, Rapid City, South Dakota, from August 2015 to March 2016, he worked closely with the President and CEO of Regional Health and the Vice President of the Regional Health Foundation to formalize all staff responsibilities, establish internal systems and controls, revise the foundation organizational chart, train and mentor existing staff, and assist in hiring new team members. In March, 2016, the President and CEO asked Frank to assume the role of President of the Regional Health Foundation on a half-time basis—ten days a month—until a full-time president was hired in late 2017.

This was his second foray in the consulting field, with his most recent full-time position being Vice President of Development for the Milwaukee School of Engineering (MSOE) for eighteen years. He was responsible for the management of all development and alumni affairs activities, marketing and public affairs, career services, mail services, and WMSE-FM. During his tenure, the university launched, completed, and exceeded the goal of its largest capital campaign in its 112-year history. The base goal was $48 million, and at completion, it raised $77 million with a fulfillment rate over 97 percent. His tenure at MSOE began in 1997 and ended in 2015 with his retirement.

Frank was with Growth Design Corporation, Milwaukee, Wisconsin, a national resource development consulting firm, for eleven years as the Managing Consultant. Prior to that, he served as the Director of Development for St. John's Northwestern Military Academy for six years with responsibilities for development, alumni and public affairs. His early career in the greater Milwaukee area started with the Next Door Foundation, Inc. as a program director for ten years.

A native of Zanesville, Ohio, Frank holds a bachelor's degree in social welfare from the University of Wisconsin-Milwaukee, and a master's degree in engineering management from the Milwaukee School of Engineering.

Frank lives in Menomonee Falls, Wisconsin, with his wife, Peggy. They have one daughter, Danielle Habib Ticcioni, who is an RN and BSN, and a granddaughter, Juliette.

CHAPTER TEN
The Improbable Major Donor
By Karen Burns

Million-dollar moments are made up of millions of moments and countless interactions that shape the donor's worldview and future philanthropic activity. This is the story of one such million-dollar moment, or multi-million-dollar moment, to be precise. It is the story of an amazing donor who changed the future of the Indianapolis Zoo and set it on a path to become a global conservation organization.

I graduated with a master's degree in nonprofit management with a concentration in philanthropy from Grand Valley State University, and have been a Certified Fundraising Executive (CFRE) since 1989.

I have been proud to serve some extraordinary organizations with transformational missions over the course of my career.

I think of myself as a connector. I put people together with ideas, needs, and solutions. In other words, I am a fundraiser. I came to the Indianapolis Zoo in 1999 from the Frederik Meijer Gardens and Sculpture Park in Grand Rapids, Michigan, where I was the Assistant Director and Chief Development Officer. One day, I received a call from an executive search firm looking for a Vice President of External Relations at the Indianapolis Zoo. The Zoo was opening a botanic garden and was looking for someone with broad not-for-profit management experience and extensive fundraising experience. This position was a perfect fit for me. I have always had a passion for animals and for zoos, and coupled with my husband's and my fondness for the City of Indianapolis, this was an easy decision to make.

The philanthropist in this story was already an integral part of the Indianapolis Zoo when I joined the team in 1999. Polly Horton Hix has a passion for wild things and wild places. I remember thinking that she could have been one of the individuals studied by Thomas Stanley and William Danko for their work *The Millionaire Next Door: The Surprising Secrets of America's Wealthy*.

If you worked with her, or stood in line with her at the grocery store, you would never suspect that she was a multimillionaire. She didn't dress in couture, drive flashy cars, live or act like a millionaire, except when it came to philanthropy. Her story is unique and her impact on the Indianapolis Zoo profound. Polly is quite simply one of the most generous and interesting people I have ever met or been privileged to know.

Her relationship with the Indianapolis Zoo began in the 1969 when she worked in the Zoo's admissions area and gift shop during college. No one back then could have predicted the extent to which this young woman would shape the future of the Indianapolis Zoo. An adopted child raised in the Chicago area, she relocated to Northern Indiana with her family when she was twelve years old. She helped care for animals on the family farm. She said that she felt out of place in her new community and school, and was more comfortable with animals than her classmates.

Polly's great grandfather founded the Chicago Bridge and Iron Works in the late 19th century in Chicago, Illinois. When her father passed away in 1973, he left a significant amount of his fortune to Polly. She said that she felt he had entrusted her with this extraordinary gift because he knew she would see the possibilities to change the world.

Polly never fit the typical profile of a major donor. While she came from a family with great wealth, she was never treated, or acted, like it. Polly served 28 years with the Marion County Sheriff's Department and retired with the rank of Major. She was good at her job, and she took it very seriously. In fact, most people who worked with Polly were unaware that Deputy Hix was a very wealthy woman and major community philanthropist.

Polly's college job at the zoo was just a few short years after it was founded in 1964, and she was one of its earliest employees. Back then, the Zoo was a 25-acre children's zoo themed around Mother Goose fables. Her experience gave her an appreciation for the day-to-day needs of zoo staff and the animals in their care. Coupled with a passion for travel, Polly had deep insight into the conditions animals were facing in the wild.

The Zoo relocated to its current downtown location in 1988 and was the first major development in the newly created White River State Park. The Zoo contributed to the rejuvenation of downtown Indianapolis, and enhanced the quality of life in Central Indiana. It was a monumental undertaking that engaged the entire community in a $64 million campaign to build the "New Zoo." Today, the Indianapolis Zoo is the largest accredited zoo in the country that receives no tax-based revenue. The Zoo relies on earned revenue and philanthropy to support its operations and growth.

In the late 1980s, very few zoos had endowments. With their reliance on city or county tax-based revenue, they either did not see the need for an endowment or were unable to create one under their operating charters. The Indianapolis Zoo was at the forefront of zoo endowments when it created the Zoological Foundation Fund in 1978 with a gift of $150,000. The endowment grew very slowly and when I arrived at the Zoo nineteen years later, it had just reached $3 million.

Polly became an annual fund donor and member of the Zoo in 1980. It was not until 1993 that she became a major donor to the Zoo, and she came along at a critical period in the Zoo's development. Following the campaign that moved the Zoo to the White River State Park, many of the traditional donors were still paying off pledges from the capital campaign, and the major gift program was not well developed.

Polly was the Zoo's angel. She was responsible for several significant exhibits and facilities at the Zoo including the state-of-the-art veterinary hospital named the Polly Horton Hix Animal Care Complex.

In 2002, the Zoo was embarking on a master plan and subsequent major gift campaign. The Board of Trustees and executive staff leadership had clear strategic direction on the future of the Zoo, and the master plan would fill in the details.

Timing for making a major gift ask is as much art as it is science. If you wait for the perfect time, you might never make the ask. If you ask too soon, you might damage your relationship with the donor and end up with either no gift, or a much smaller gift than might otherwise have been received. Timing was an important factor in this gift request.

Zoo President and CEO Jeffrey Bonner, PhD, had been instrumental in building the Zoo's major donor base and was very close to Polly, and had just resigned to accept a position as President and CEO of the St. Louis Zoo. The new CEO had not yet been named, and there was a lot of concern about the momentum for the campaign and for the institution.

The Indianapolis Zoo was heading in a new direction. In addition to the Zoo serving the community as a much-loved attraction, it was gaining national prominence for its work in animal conservation and welfare. It was critical that we kept the momentum going and positioned the organization for success during the leadership transition. The center was the cornerstone of the vision for the future of the Indianapolis Zoo.

Internally at the Zoo, we had discussed making a major gift request to Polly for the Center for several months prior to the CEO's resignation. I knew we were on solid ground with the vision for the gift, and it was unclear how long it would take for a new CEO to be named. I felt strongly that the time was right for both the donor and the institution to ask for this commitment. Waiting six months to a year for the new CEO to get fully acquainted with the donor might have pushed the request into a less favorable window for the donor to make this big of a commitment. There was risk with either decision, but I felt the benefit of obtaining this transformational gift on behalf of the institution outweighed the potential downside.

Paul Grayson was the acting CEO during the transition and had known Polly for over twenty years. We both had strong relationships with her, which convinced me to propose to Paul that we ask Polly to consider making a significant endowment gift to create a conservation and research center at the Indianapolis Zoo.

Paul Grayson and I met with Polly in 2002 and laid out the following vision:

The Polly Horton Hix Institute for Research and Conservation

Over the last two decades, zoos, and other conservation-oriented organizations have developed a broad and powerful strategy for conserving endangered species worldwide. Termed the "flagship species" approach, this strategy is based on the notion that if we focus on saving a single, very charismatic species, and save the habitat in which that species is found, we can save all the other plants and animals that make up that habitat.

We must do everything in our power to ensure that the Zoo, first, continues the vital work mandated by the board and, second, meets with the greatest success possible in these efforts. We do not embark on these efforts for the national and international acclaim that they will yield. We do not do this solely to key our education, fundraising, marketing, and exhibition programs. We do not do this merely to inspire our local community and involve them in globally significant conservation activities. We do these things because they will, if done completely and well, result in broad, pervasive, and meaningful transformations of our natural world. We believe that we can change the world. Not all of it, and not all at once, but we can make a profound difference.

We are proposing the creation of an Institute within the Zoo that will be dedicated to facilitating our rapidly growing research and conservation efforts. The goals of this institute will be to ensure that we will have the resources, in terms of staff, facilities, and funding, to undertake a small number of internationally significant research and conservation efforts; to ensure that these efforts will have the maximum impact on the conservation of flagship species and the habitats in which they are found; and to sustain existing long-term efforts while judiciously expanding the number of new efforts to be undertaken in years to come.

The cornerstone of the Institute must be a dedicated endowment. The funds from this endowment will be used not only to fund existing and new efforts but, more importantly, to provide seed money to move specific projects forward to the point that other funding sources become a realistic possibility.

The request was to establish and name the new institute. Polly's reaction was immediate and positive. She was excited about the vision and agreed on the spot to talk to her financial team about the idea. She is passionate about education and conservation, and believed the proposed Institute was the perfect way to begin to change the future. Polly is a sophisticated philanthropist who uses her intellect, but always gives from the heart and always with the motivation of leaving a legacy worthy of her father and family. It was the largest single gift from an individual in the Zoo's history.

I experienced several emotions when she committed to this remarkable gift, the first and foremost was awe. Awe at knowing that I was at the very beginning of a very significant venture that had the power to change the world, and awe at knowing I had just witnessed the joyful giving of a sacrificial gift. In fundraising, we talk about sacrificial giving. Sacrificial giving requires careful financial planning and is motivated by gratitude for the gifts one has received in their lives. That describes Polly.

The Polly H. Hix Institute for Research and Conservation was established in 2003 and has provided the impetus for major conservation initiatives such as the Indianapolis Prize and the Zoo's Conservation Grant Program that annually awards grants to scientists who are actively engaged in field research and conservation work around the globe.

In the fourteen years since its creation, the Hix Institute has evolved into a catalyst to influence individuals to act to advance animal conservation. The Zoo is uniquely positioned to advance animal conservation and to stem the ever-growing rate of extinction by changing the way in which people view animals and the natural world.

The Institute leverages education and conservation connections to influence people's attitudes, opinions, and actions. It fosters connections between guests and wildlife, the kind of connections that make an impression and inspire change, and it does this by creating connections between Hoosiers and conservationists worldwide. The Hix Institute connects Hoosiers, regional, national, and international visitors, with the daily adventures, victories, and challenges of the heroes who are saving wildlife all over the world, while presenting memorable encounters with the amazing creatures with which we share our planet.

Because of this transformational gift, we can envision a future where the city of Indianapolis becomes a conservation hub and home to one of the world's most influential conservation organizations. The gift set in motion a new understanding of what it means to be a Zoo at the forefront of global conservation.

Polly has been a major force in elevating the Indianapolis Zoo to an internationally recognized global conservation organization. She has dedicated herself to making the world a better place—through her career with the Marion County Sheriff's Department and through her philanthropy. Polly has left an indelible footprint on Indianapolis. In addition to the Zoo, she has made significant gifts to the Children's Museum of Indianapolis, the Indiana State Museum, the Eiteljorg Museum, and the University of Indianapolis, to name a few.

The gift that led to the Hix Institute was 50 years in the making, and started with a young girl's love of animals and a summer job at the Zoo. The foundation for my million-dollar moment was laid long before anyone suspected that Polly Hix would donate millions of dollars in total to the Indianapolis Zoo over the course of 37 years. It is a potent reminder that significant donors come from surprising places, and he or she may be standing right next to you wearing a staff or volunteer uniform. You cannot always identify the millionaire or future millionaire in the room. Every person and every interaction on behalf of your organization can be a form of cultivation.

As fundraisers, it is our job to listen carefully for clues to an individual's motivations and inclinations. We are entrusted with being the messenger for our institutions and explaining how a donor can make a difference with his or her gift. It is our role to move relationships to the point of solicitation, and to identify the sweet spot for the purpose, amount, and timing of the specific request. This is where the "art" of fundraising comes in. Sometimes you need to be bold and rely on your intuition when working with a donor. If there is one thing we know for sure in fundraising, it's if you don't make the ask, you are unlikely to get the gift.

The gift to establish the Polly H. Hix Institute for Research and Conservation was not the first million-dollar gift I have been a part of, nor was it the last. But it was the largest gift from an individual I had ever secured, and it is among the most far reaching and important gifts of my career.

About Karen Burns

Burns

Karen Burns is a seasoned non-for-profit executive with extensive hands-on fundraising leadership in capital campaigns and all facets of nonprofit leadership.

Graduating magna cum laude with a bachelor of science from Western Michigan University, Karen obtained a master in public administration from Grand Valley State University in Allendale, Michigan. She has been a Certified Fundraising Executive since 1996.

Karen began her professional fundraising career with the March of Dimes Birth Defects Foundation in Louisville, Kentucky. She spent seven years with the March of Dimes, ultimately becoming the Executive Director of the Northwest Ohio Chapter in Toledo, Ohio. She went on to serve as the Director of Alumni Relations at The University of Toledo for three years before moving to Grand Rapids, Michigan, with her husband. She served as the Assistant Director of the Frederik Meijier Gardens and Sculpture Park in Grand

Rapids, before moving to Indianapolis, Indiana to accept her dream position with the Indianapolis Zoo.

Karen is Executive Vice President of the Indianapolis Zoological Society and Executive Director of the Indianapolis Prize. She has been with the Zoo since 1999 and has direct responsibility for key management areas, including institutional advancement, membership, marketing, creative services, public relations, education, conservation and the Indianapolis Prize.

In her role with the Zoo, Karen led the team that conducted a comprehensive rebranding of the Zoo from a much-loved community attraction into a world-class conservation institution.

Karen also heads up the Indianapolis Prize, a significant initiative of the Zoo's mission to empower people and communities to advance animal conservation. Established in 2005, the Prize has grown to become the world's leading award for animal conservation, awarding $250,000 to the winner and $10,000 to each of the five finalists.

Active in the community, Karen was named one of the Indianapolis Business Journal's Women of Influence in 2014. She serves on the Board of the Kiwanis Foundation of Indianapolis, is immediate past President of the Downtown Indy Marketing Board, and serves on the Downtown Indy Board of Directors. She also serves as Vice-Chairman of the Advisory Board of the Salvation Army Indiana Division.

Karen and her husband, Rick Gevers, live in downtown Indianapolis with one very cranky cat.

CHAPTER ELEVEN

An Anniversary Gift

By Gene Tempel
Founding Dean Emeritus and Professor of Philanthropic Studies, Indiana University Lilly
Family School of Philanthropy
Persident Emeritus, Indiana University Foundation

My philanthropic autobiography begins when our home burned to the ground in 1954. All of our personal effects and belongings were destroyed. I remember the outpouring of support from friends, neighbors, and the entire community, wanting to help make our lives whole again. I never lost my fascination with the phenomenon of philanthropy. I decided early in my career not only to practice fundraising as "the servant of philanthropy" described by Hank Rosso,[4] but to understand it better. That quest for understanding led to the founding of the Indiana University (IU) Center on Philanthropy, and ultimately, to the founding of the IU Lilly Family School of Philanthropy.

After 30 years, we now know much more about the philanthropic impulse than we did then. In several studies of high net worth households, the belief in the mission or cause is the most important factor in making a gift. According to *The 2016 U.S. Trust Study of High Net Worth Philanthropy,* written and researched by the Lilly Family School of Philanthropy, high net worth households are typically the source of million-dollar-plus gifts.[5] "Belief in the cause" echoes Rosso's "fundraising is the servant of philanthropy." The case for support is the most important aspect of soliciting a million dollar gift. Rosso also said, "Fundraising is the gentle art of teaching the joy of giving!"[6] Research has shown that donors and volunteers experience pleasure from giving and volunteering.[7] These things are important to my million-dollar moment. Perhaps the most important aspect of my million-dollar moment is captured in my own reminder that fundraising is the difficult work of engaging others in your cause. Million-dollar moments typically result from engagement of the donor over time to develop deep commitment to the cause, trust in the organization, and

85

awareness of the impact or difference that the gift will make.

I have been involved in a number of million-dollar gifts during my career. I have seen colleagues in my organization engage million-dollar donors as well. The strategy of soliciting the gift usually has been built on years of engagement and understanding of how the donor's values supported the cause or particular program. In my case, that has involved million-dollar gifts for a theatre, two Benedictine communities, other nonprofit organizations, and Indiana University. In all cases of which I am familiar, million-dollar gifts were the result of a deep belief in the cause, long involvement of the donor with the organization, and a feeling of satisfaction and joy on the part of the donor.

I spent most of my professional career working for Indiana University. Part of that time was spent on the IU campus in Bloomington, part on the Indiana University-Purdue University Indianapolis (IUPUI) campus. No matter what position I held, I was always involved in fundraising. At an organization as large and complex as IU, most million-dollar donors are engaged with a particular program or location.

After serving in a variety of administrative roles, I found myself leading the development of the IU Center on Philanthropy which I had helped found in 1987. One of the primary responsibilities of the position was fundraising and continued development of contracts for research and services. The benefit to all of philanthropy was an enhanced understanding of philanthropy, donor motivations, trends, fundraising, and the whole of issues that impacted philanthropy and the nonprofit sector. Success in funding led IU to become the national and international leader in research, academic programs, and professional training related to nonprofits, philanthropy, and fundraising training.

In 2008, I was appointed President of the IU Foundation. One of the responsibilities of this position is to provide leadership for a university-wide development team covering eight campuses. I participated in, or celebrated the success of, colleagues for the naming of two law schools, a school of public health, the Lilly Family School of Philanthropy, and the naming of a new facility for the Kelley School of Business, as well as dozens of endowed chairs and programs, all at the million-dollar plus level during my time as President.

But my favorite million-dollar moment is not a story of strategy in putting together a solicitation team or preparing the perfect proposal to capture a donor's interests. Rather it is the story of how deep engagement of a husband and wife in various aspects of the university led to an unsolicited gift to one of her deepest interests.

Gary Anderson, MD, is a former intern, resident, and fellow of the IU School of Medicine who had a successful career as a physician, and subsequently, a venture capitalist in Philadelphia. Kathy Ziliak Anderson is a graduate of the IU School of Nursing who committed much of her volunteer time to the Pennsylvania Ballet. After retirement, Gary and Kathy relocated to Nashville, Indiana, twenty miles from Bloomington, where both became involved with IU as volunteers. They are both deeply engaged with the Jacobs School of Music. Gary also participates as a member of the IU Foundation Board with special service on the Board's Investment Committee and several other committees. Additionally, he has been engaged as a member of the Kelley School of Business Dean's Advisory Council and the Executive Committee of the Johnson Center for Entrepreneurship and Innovation, and other volunteer activities. In addition to being a founding member of the Women's Philanthropy Leadership Council, Kathy has also been involved with the IU Alumni Association, the Women's Colloquium Steering Committee, and the Jacobs School Friends of Music.

One day when I was the IU Foundation President, I noticed a meeting with Gary on my calendar. When he arrived for his appointment, after the usual pleasantries, he asked, "What does it cost to endow a chair?" I replied, "$1.5 million." I assumed that we were going to have a policy discussion about the cost of endowing a chair. Instead he said, "I would like to set up an endowed chair in Kathy's name for our 35th wedding anniversary. After taking a few moments to process the news, I responded with, "That's a great idea!"

The conversation that followed focused on two important aspects of any million-dollar moment: remember to agree on the details for fulfilling the gift and determine a meaningful purpose for the gift. The conversation reflected an important aspect of philanthropy that we understand from research today, that making a meaningful gift brings fulfillment to the donor. Coming to agreement on the terms of the gift was easy. The gift would be made as a pledge and paid in five pledge payments, with an option to pay fully if financial circumstances made that advantageous. That provided information for the first part of the gift agreement.

Determining the most meaningful purpose for his spouse meant doing a philanthropic autobiography for and doing discernment with another person. We discussed options for carrying out this conversation, and agreed to meet again in a week after he had time to have careful conversations with Kathy without ruining the surprise.

Since Gary and Kathy were deeply involved with the Jacobs School of Music, that was a natural focus. And since Kathy had a special involvement with ballet at IU and in Philadelphia, ballet became the specific program of interest. That anniversary gift became the Kathy Ziliak Anderson Chair in Ballet, the first endowed chair in classical ballet in the country. There was joy all around: Gary, Kathy, the dean, the chairholder, and me.

The experience reminded me that we as fundraisers often assign ourselves credit for "million-dollar moments," when the credit for success is the credibility of our organizations and the case for support that allows donors to say, "I gave because I believed in the cause!" If we and our colleagues can take credit for anything, often it is our ability to design meaningful activities that engage potential donors. It is our ability to help our CEOs and others in the organization to take seriously transparency and accountability to help build trust among our donors and prospects. If we engage them in our work, they will know the funding priorities, they will know the impact their gifts can have, and they will be comfortable discussing million-dollar gifts. That is the real "million-dollar moment."

About Eugene R. Tempel

Tempel

Professor Tempel is Founding Dean Emeritus and Professor of Philanthropic Studies of the Indiana University Lilly Family School of Philanthropy, and President Emeritus of the Indiana University Foundation. He led the world's first school devoted to research and teaching about philanthropy. An internationally recognized expert on the philanthropic sector, he has four decades of leadership and fundraising experience. He helped found the school's precursor, the Center on Philanthropy, and was its executive director for eleven years, transforming it into a leading national resource.

Generous donors recently established the Eugene R. Tempel Endowed Deanship at the school to honor Professor Tempel. It will enable future deans to continue the development of the Lilly Family School of Philanthropy to reach its full potential, and to achieve its goal of improving philanthropy to improve the world.

A member of several nonprofit boards, Professor Tempel is a past chair of the National Association of Fundraising Professionals' Ethics Committee. An early leader in creating the field of philanthropic studies, he was the first elected president of the Nonprofit Academic Centers Council and a member of Independent Sector's Expert Advisory Panel that helped create national guidelines for nonprofit governance and ethical behavior.

The author of several works in the field, he has won numerous awards and has been named among the 50 most influential nonprofit sector leaders thirteen times by The NonProfit Times, which also named him the sector's first "Influencer of the Year" in 2013.

He earned a bachelor's degree in English and philosophy from St. Benedict College, a master degree in English, and a doctorate in higher education administration from Indiana University.

Professor Tempel was born on a farm in Southern Indiana and is a first generation college graduate. He learned philanthropy at an early age through neighbor helping neighbor when fire destroyed his family's home. He and his wife Mary, a nurse practitioner, are volunteer fundraisers. They have lived in Indianapolis, Indiana, since 1983. They have three adult sons, Jonathan, Jason, and Zachary and three grandchildren, Sydney, Sophie, and Bo.

CHAPTER TWELVE
Our Chairman, Our Champion
By Kathleen Carroll

"We are the music-makers, and we are the dreamers of dreams…"
—Arthur O'Shaunessy

It was a million-dollar moment for the Toledo Symphony in the early 1990s when Richard P. Anderson agreed to chair the campaign to raise $20 million for the endowment. It felt like the sun was coming up to welcome a brand-new day.

At that time, symphony costs were increasing and operating income from earned and contributed revenue was declining. Dick Anderson accepted leadership of an effort that would essentially save the orchestra. A veteran fundraiser, he understood the challenge of the effort. As a music lover, he understood and appreciated the value added to the community by its resident orchestra.

Dick was then Managing Partner of The Andersons, a family-owned agricultural business with deep roots in Maumee, Ohio, just outside of Toledo. He is the youngest son of the founder, Harold Anderson, who started the company in 1947. Initially, the company's businesses were based in grain storage and fertilizer. The Andersons had a reputation for building enduring relationships and possessing a knack for finding new ways to add value.

Background—This Is Where I Came In

I joined the staff of the Toledo Orchestra Association, Inc. (The Toledo Symphony) as Director of Development and Public Relations in the fall of 1988, just as the Symphony's 45th season commenced. I was the first experienced professional to hold this position, and I was eager to learn about music.

In four decades, from 1943 to 1983, this regional symphony orchestra was already noteworthy for the quality of its music performances. The Toledo Symphony was then, and still is, known in American music circles for its exemplary "on the road" outreach to communities across Northwest Ohio and Southeast Michigan, which included music education for school children and their families.

As the orchestra developed, it distinguished itself for changing its compensation practice from "per service" (hourly) pay to salaried positions, modeling the practice of orchestras in major metropolitan areas. It was predictable that more musicians from across the country competed for positions with the Toledo Symphony. They moved into the community to build careers in music, and in doing so, they enriched the character of the community.

In return for a regular salary, management retained discretion over the use of service hours, which could be used for a great variety of performance, entertainment, and educational needs from full orchestra to small ensembles. The orchestra became the "one-stop shop" for music. This dense schedule of musical activities merited the orchestra's claim of "525 performances in 365 days," and the Symphony became known as one of the hardest working orchestras in America.

When I arrived, the operating budget was $3.5 million. The endowment of less than $2 million was being used to fund the initiation of the comprehensive development program I was to direct. Our goal was to raise an endowment ten times that size. Equally important was my responsibility to plan and manage a comprehensive development program to fund the operating budget.

Like most of the people working in nonprofit financial development offices, I had worked in small to mid-size nonprofit organizations learning the fundamentals of good development on-the-job. I had taken advantage of training at conferences and workshops. I had become adept over two decades in the profession in all the building blocks of development; however, fundraising for an orchestra was going to be unique.

In my career I learned to be a self-starter. There was rarely sufficient staff, so achieving success required reliance on volunteers and the strength of my relationships with them. Everything I did in development was grounded in the belief that people give money to people for the benefit of other people. Major and capital gifts needed to be cultivated and solicited by people. Keeping a cadre of dependable volunteers was an absolute necessity wherever I worked. It was of importance that leadership from the ranks of trustees, long-time major donors, and friends was engaged in the fundraising process if it were going to achieve its objectives.

The Growing Financial Need

In the two decades before I arrived, the orchestra's music product and community service improved steadily. Artistically, the broad attraction and retention of musicians and conductors had resulted in the hiring of more proficient players. The orchestra sounded better, driving growth in both audiences and donors. Yet, the operating budget fell into chronic undercapitalization, resulting in deficits. Deficits create institutional stress, and drive a need to make changes. The choices were to generate a stable source of funding, or face severe structural change.

Tools for Change

Over the years, the Toledo Symphony had grown its governing board from music lovers and teachers to one comprised of top community business and civic leaders, adding acknowledged arts patrons with financial resources who understood the cultural life of the community. A strong and loyal core of individual patrons subscribed annually and donated regularly. In addition, there was a long-standing auxiliary organization, the Toledo Symphony League, which hosted major fundraising events, and provided volunteers to participate in the Symphony's educational programs. Needed was a key volunteer to embrace the effort to capitalize the Toledo Symphony Endowment Fund. We searched for "the right person, for the right job at the right time." It took some time, but we found him.

The unanimous choice was Richard P. Anderson, President and CEO, The Andersons, Inc., who had joined the Board of Trustees out of concern for the long-term sustainability of music in the regional community. He had learned to love music from his mother, Margaret, and realized that a fine orchestra was a tremendous personal and community resource. A recognized leader, Dick came from a family known for decades of community service.

Although initially reluctant to accept the responsibility, Dick realized he had the passion, skills, and influence to secure the Symphony's financial future. He made a commitment to the work of the endowment program. The Chairman championed the musicians he so admired, and considered them to be essential campaign partners. Most fundraising appointments included music in some form. He devoted time from his crushing schedule to strategize with staff and meet with donors to share the Symphony's success and challenges. Dick was committed to do the work that would add $20 million to the endowment by the year 2000. Utterly reliable, he got the job done.

Being "On a Roll"

Early on, looking for donor peers, Dick Anderson represented the Symphony's case for support personally to a local family foundation, asking for a gift of $1 million to honor the legacy of the Founders of the Toledo Symphony, one of whom was the matriarch of the family a generation earlier. It was Dick who captured the foundation's interest and encouraged them to join him in shaping a future for music in the region. They agreed to participate.

The chairman was able to articulate to the corporate and individual donor community appreciation for the unique role performed by the musicians of the Toledo Symphony. The momentum was growing.

As the capital effort moved forward, a remarkable stimulus grant was made to the Toledo Symphony from the Mellon Foundation's Orchestra Program. It provided transformational funding of more than $2 million over the next decade to support the growth and development of the Toledo Symphony through initiatives which would benefit musician careers, the community, and the endowment. This was a momentous partnership which had profound impact on the Symphony's image. The validation that accompanied this grant was priceless.

It was a heady time of unprecedented support. True to his generous nature, Dick Anderson credited all success to trustees, donors, friends, and musicians who achieved the financial victory.

What We Learned

The right leader is worth the wait. It is essentially the biggest gift you can give to a campaign. If a good choice is made, the leader provides knowledge, wisdom, and an impassioned commitment that propels the fundraising operation forward. Dick Anderson was honest, believable, and made and sold an enthusiastic case for support. Working with him was an exceptional experience. His sense of humor made disappointing decisions bearable, and he was always willing to return to an indecisive prospect for further discussion. He was a hands-on leader who juggled a myriad of responsibilities serving his business, community, family, and faith. Yet, Dick had the ability to make you feel that your interests were first in line. In turn, our successes stimulated pride among the musicians who could feel the community's embrace.

The year 1998 was a noteworthy time of financial peace. The endowment was growing. Operating deficits abated. The audience was growing, and donors were increasingly responsive. It was a very good time for music, and the arrival of music leadership from the new principal conductor.

Since then, much has changed in our common culture. The arts, especially the musical arts, face adaptation to digital reality.

What remains unchanged, as we learned, are the ingredients to create the success of a major financial effort: an institution with a history of excellence; a well-conceived plan of action; and, committed and knowledgeable leadership with a team of dedicated volunteers.

Also unchanged is the essential character of the live performance of orchestral masterpieces. These works of art require the same music force as they did when they were composed. The duration of each composition has remained constant over time. Access to live music performances has increased significantly with digital technology. Still, the performance of a music masterpiece experienced in the company of others remains a singular and exceptional event.

About Kathleen Carroll

Carroll

Kathleen Carroll retired in 2016 as President and CEO of the Toledo Orchestra Association (The Toledo Symphony), a position she held since 2010. Prior to assuming this position, she was the Symphony's Executive Vice President of Development. She initially joined the staff as Director of Development and Public Relations in 1988.

During three decades with this regional orchestra serving communities across Northwest Ohio and Southeast Michigan, she initiated the development and implementation of strategic and comprehensive advancement and communications programs, including annual fund campaigns, foundation grants and sponsorships, special events, capital campaigns and major and planned gift programs. During that time more than $70 million was generated to support performance and education programs designed to enrich, entertain, and educate the broad community. These resource development efforts enabled the Toledo Symphony to enhance its reputation for the artistic quality of its performances and its uncommon level of community service

Kathleen was recognized with the prestigious YWCA Milestone Award for the Arts in 2005. It was during her tenure as President and CEO that the Toledo Symphony made its Carnegie Hall debut in the inaugural "Spring for Music" Festival in 2011. The following season a chorus of nearly 1,000 youngsters was assembled for the orchestra's debut Huntington Center performance of Beethoven's Symphony No. 9.

Prior to joining the Toledo Symphony, Ms. Carroll was principal in Kathleen Carroll and Associates with clients in healthcare and public education. Previously she developed the advancement program at Maumee Valley Country Day School, initiated a planned giving program for the St. Vincent Hospital Foundation (both located in Toledo), served as an associate of the Station Independence Program for the Public Broadcasting Service (PBS) based in Washington, DC, managed fundraising and communications programs for WGTE-TV/ FM Toledo Public Broadcasting, and worked as producer and host of WOHO-WXEZ Toledo commercial radio programs.

Kathleen was a founding member of the Toledo Chapter of the National Society of Fundraising Executives, serving as president in subsequent years. She was a fellow at the Executive Leadership Institute (ELI) at Indiana University Center for Philanthropy, and was selected to participate in the Mellon Foundation Orchestra Leadership Program through the League of American Orchestras. An active member of the Rotary Club of Toledo, she served on many nonprofit boards.

Kathleen and her husband, Carl White, live in Ottawa Hills, Ohio. They are the parents of four adult children and four grandsons.

CHAPTER THIRTEEN
Body, Mind, and Spirit
By Kenneth L. Gladish, PhD

In 1960, a small group of community leaders in the North Shore suburbs of Chicago rallied around a young YMCA executive, Ken Thiel, who was committed to establishing a new YMCA to serve the kids and families of the area. The Rotary Clubs in these suburbs that would be served by the new YMCA became active sponsors of this idea. Men and women who had grown up with their local Ys became early leaders of this movement. The YMCA of Evanston, Illinois, supported the effort as an outreach to other towns and villages on the North Shore of Chicago.

By 1966, Ken had made enough progress building membership and programs that the next logical step was to consider a capital campaign to support construction of a YMCA facility in Northbrook, Illinois. Under his leadership, wide ranging youth and family programs had flourished using a multitude of community facilities to serve a growing membership and participant body. Generous churches, the Jewish Community Center, schools, parks, and other YMCAs had hosted this new young entity which would come to be known as the North Suburban YMCA.

A case had been made that the communities involved could benefit by the permanent presence of a YMCA. This was true even though these communities were served by robust and innovative public park districts. Supporters argued that a new YMCA facility could be positioned as a powerful addition of services and programs not offered by others.

For the times, this was not an unusual pattern of development for a new YMCA. Since the 1850s, YMCAs have spread, grown and flourished precisely because of the core commitment of local volunteers supported by neighboring YMCAs and a robust national YMCA resource system. As is the case today, every YMCA is an independent, locally supported, public charity, reliant on local initiative, local financial support, and local volunteers, engaged with YMCA professional staff leaders. This was true in Northbrook, and remains so more than 50 years later.

My parents had decided to move to Northbrook from Evanston in 1953. It just so happened that Ken Thiel and his wife, Alta, moved to the same street just a couple of years later, as Ken's career as a YMCA professional was getting under full sail as a program executive at the Evanston YMCA. The two young couples had met through mutual friends who also soon migrated to the same street in Northbrook.

Interestingly, my father, Hjalmer Gladish, had benefitted from the Evanston McGaw YMCA's program as a boy growing up in Evanston. He came from a working class family with limited economic resources, which struggled financially during the Great Depression. Even before the Depression, his family found it difficult to thrive. To help support his family, he had worked in various odd jobs since he was nine years old. This work included collecting recyclable paper and cans, helping his mother provide laundry services to the "big houses" of close by neighborhoods, and setting up a newsstand at the corner of Chicago Avenue and Main Street in Evanston. He operated this newsstand from about 1930 through the early 1950s, even through the Second World War when he was serving in the US Navy overseas.

Generous donors in Evanston supported a summer camp scholarship program for financially disadvantaged children at the Y's Camp Echo, a terrific facility in Fremont, Michigan. My father was one of the children who benefitted from the scholarship program in the late 1920s. He was able to attend the camp each summer from the age of ten to twelve years old. All of his transportation, equipment, participation, and residential costs were supported by loyal Evanston Y donors. Even today, the YMCA takes appropriate pride in its aspiration to turn no one away because of an inability to pay. The roots of my own family's devotion to the YMCA can be traced to my father's ability to attend summer camp in his youth. By the time my parents were residents in Northbrook, they made every effort to support the new YMCA and their neighbor's work within the admittedly limited resources they had available.

Ken Thiel and the small group of volunteers he had recruited were following the classic handbook approach to YMCA development in a new community. This was a historically proven approach that had been refined over the years, and was proving to be a success once again. The national YMCA's wholly owned capital campaign consultancy, CAMPAIGN Associates, sent one of its top campaign executives to shepherd the project. An office was established, teams were organized, and the fundraising effort was underway.

Not coincidentally, my mother, Edyth Gladish, served as one of the campaign's two volunteer secretarial assistants. While the pair of them worked in offices in Northbrook's only multi-story downtown commercial building, the Y's own management offices were located in a cramped basement office space under a hair salon across the street from Village Green Park, in what passed for downtown Northbrook. Ken was nothing if not frugal. I had started my own youthful career serving as the weekend custodian in that basement office, no mean task in a space dominated by a large and sometimes smoke-belching furnace apparatus.

As students of fundraising history in the United States know, the Y helped create the modern practice of community-based capital and annual support campaigns. The Y was a very early practitioner, developing systems, strategies, and tactics that would be widely adopted and adapted by America's charitable sector. In addition to America's religious congregations, colleges, and universities, the Y could rightfully be credited with setting the pattern for the future of fundraising from the late 19th century through the post war era in the arena of community fundraising. This impact grew through the Y's participation in the development of community funds, including Community Chests, United Ways and other collective fundraising structures.

This pioneering work also helped give birth to the start of a professional field of practice in fundraising. In addition to its wholly owned fundraising department, the Y also used its capable national training system to educate YMCA professional leaders in the art of fundraising. The Y also helped produce an early generation of independent fundraising professionals. Many of these mostly male practitioners had previous career experience with the Y. Quite a bit of the early history of what would become the country's preeminent fundraising firms was written by YMCA-trained and experienced professionals.

While the Y has, since its American founding in 1851, depended upon fundraising success, the discipline and focus on best practice has waxed and waned over a century and half of history. In the early part of the 21st Century, the Y and its leaders have created a bit of a renaissance in fundraising. The Y's tri-national (USA, Canada, Mexico) North American YMCA Development Organization, is a vital, effective, and fully embraced source of training, recognition, research, and best practice.

This is also a time in which the Y has made excellence in philanthropy a major pillar of its hope for growth and progress in service to American communities. There is even an effort afoot to create a national fundraising platform building alongside rebranding efforts and collective programmatic initiatives. The annual reports of the "Philanthropy 400" of *The Chronicle of Philanthropy* have perennially positioned combined YMCA annual fundraising as among the top ten nonprofit achievements for decades. There is a strong belief that this achievement can, and should, be enhanced.

An important part of every YMCA Campaign of the mid-20th century era was active involvement of "youth spokespersons." These were young people who had experienced the impact of Y programs and could tell a good story. This is a practice, which persists, happily, to this day in many YMCA communities.

I was selected to be one of these young people for the North Suburban YMCA campaign from 1967 through 1969. What better way to access and influence support for fundraising goals than to feature recipients and beneficiaries of the generosity of others? Personal testimony can engage the head and the heart of potential donors, and is a proven element in building a compelling case for support. No other element has as big an impact on connecting interested donors to cause.

My selection as one of a few Youth Spokesmen was probably due to a number of factors. Of course, I was well-known to the YMCA's executive leader. He was a neighbor, friend, and trusted community presence. He thought I would do well as a spokesman, and that I would learn much from the experience. Like most Y executives of the era, he had an innate interest in youth development, a lot of experience serving children and their families, and a genuine interest in making a difference day-by-day, kid-by-kid.

One other element probably played into my selection. By 1967, I had become an active student and competitor in high school debate and speech contests. Through these programs, I was learning what an effective spoken presentation was and how to best deliver it in a variety of settings.

It was also true that I had been an enthusiastic and actively engaged participant in a wide range of the programs offered by the Y as it developed since its founding days in Northbrook. I was also, as previously noted, the weekend custodian of the Y's offices.

I could not have guessed, more than 50 years ago, that fate would join to give me a very early exposure to elements of a career as a volunteer and professional fundraiser that would last a lifetime. From eighth grade on, I became engaged in the intimate, compelling, challenging, and meaningful work of fundraising for worthy causes as both a volunteer and a professional.

It was in the capital campaign for the YMCA in Northbrook that I would get my first exposure to the exhilaration of success as part of a team responsible for securing major gifts. Of course, I would not have known the language of fundraising, the distinctive tools of the professional fundraiser or the solicitation strategies practiced by true professionals. I did know my YMCA, however, and I knew it was doing a good thing in my life and the lives of many other youth in its service area.

I also had the encouragement of my parents, and their pride in knowing the fact that I was, in some small way, paying it forward. The lessons learned in that very early experience have remained with me ever since. In the thinking of the times, John Kennedy's persuasive recitation adopted from the Gospel of Luke, Chapter 12 "To whom much is given, much is required," remained a powerful call to action.

Kennedy included this call in his January 9, 1961, pre-inaugural address to the Massachusetts Legislature.

In that same speech, Kennedy asserted that the court of history would measure his administration and leaders of the time on the basis of answers to four questions. These questions would inquire, at some future time, whether leaders of his era were men of courage, judgement, integrity, and dedication.

These characteristics could as easily have been incorporated into the YMCA's aspiration for the desired impact of its programs on the lives of its members and program participants. Years later, as the Y developed its program to spread a set of core character traits in its character development initiative, the Y committed itself to the explicit promotion of the characteristics of caring, honesty, respect, responsibility, and faith. These were not the mere synthetic products of a marketing exercise. Rather, they were a distillation of the real history and historic aspirations that lay at the heart of YMCA work for a century and a half in North America.

Because of this, it was not all particularly hard for a young advocate to connect to the persuasive core of the YMCA's work, to talk about its impact on his life, and to invite powerful adults to support the cause. It was also not a giant leap to connect contemporary donors to such ideas.

A Community Arises

About the same time the YMCA development in Northbrook was gaining momentum, changes were afoot in the community itself. A classic post-war suburban community, Northbrook had been a bedroom suburb for most of the 1950s and early 1960s. Before that, it had been a largely semi-rural, exurban farm town and train stop for the Milwaukee Railroad. Northbrook's neighboring towns shared a similar history.

In the mid-1960s, a number of major enterprises and business operations decided to locate within, and contiguous to, the Northbrook village limits. This development was due, in part, to the construction of Interstate 294. The new expressway offered ease of access to the suburbs along the Chicago's far west side as well as the suburbs hugging the Lake Michigan coastline north of the city. The highway also offered a new access point to O'Hare Airport, which helped make it one of the world's busiest, and an important magnet for locating mid-continent corporate operations close to its burgeoning services.

The western boundary of Northbrook straddled the new tollway amidst open fields and farmlands, ripe for development. At the same time, the farms fringing the Northbrook village core were fast developing into new and more expensive housing tracts for both city commuters and the suburban workforce. This was also true for the other core suburbs that would be served by the new North Suburban YMCA.

Among the new enterprises attracted to this developing geography were both national and local businesses. Perhaps the most important, and certainly the largest, was Allstate Insurance Company. It had purchased a significant tract of land on both sides of the toll way on the west side of Northbrook where the Old Willow Road now crossed over the toll way. In 1967, Allstate opened its new national headquarters on an expansive corporate campus with a signature building and great plans for growth and expansion. It found corporate companions among other businesses, including Zenith Radio Corporation, A.C. Nielsen, Culligan Inc., and others. Fifty years later, Allstate is still growing on that well-developed corporate campus.

Employees followed their companies, with many migrating to the suburbs as well. Company executives especially helped lead this expansion. This new generation was building families, joining religious congregations, engaging in civic associations, active in local politics and schools, and motivated to join and lead in a multitude of ways. In this, these new residents were characteristic of the men and women of what has come to be called the "greatest generation."

One can imagine that an ambitious, energetic, and persuasive young YMCA executive would have made every effort to enlist local leaders in his ambitious goal to build a new YMCA. His professional and personal interests coincided well with the aspirations of those seeking to build businesses, and contribute to strong communities where families would be the beneficiaries of excellence in every dimension of their shared lives.

While the businesses around Northbrook were developing, a coincident growth was happening in community organizations and charitable institutions. Northbrook's schools, library, village government, park district, and related entities were growing and thriving. Likewise, the village's charitable organizations were also flourishing. The buildings, programs, and membership of religious congregations, civic associations, service clubs, youth groups, and others were enjoying the benefits of population growth, burgeoning affluence, and high aspiration.

One of these new entrants to civic life in Northbrook was a recently planted congregation of the Swedish Covenant Church. Rooted in Scandinavian traditions of evangelical Christian Protestantism, the church is now as present in American life as the Evangelical Covenant Church. It came to Northbrook, purchasing more than 60 acres of former farmland in the southern range of the village. The church had high aspirations for this property. It sought to develop and build a new church sanctuary and education facility to serve congregants from the neighborhoods of the city of Chicago and beyond. It also wanted to grow its membership and active community of worshippers. This effort was led by a core group of future congregants who were intent on making Northbrook their new home for residence, worship, education, and service.

The congregation's plans for the land were ambitious, and far surpassed building a new church and congregational center. Plans also included construction of a retirement village to serve both congregants and the general public. It would give easy access to the church life of the congregation occupying a quadrant of the land for those who were so inclined. The Swedish Covenant Church had many years experience developing and managing retirement centers. Today, there are fifteen retirement centers affiliated with the church. Northbrook's Covenant Village is one of them.

In the 1960s, Northbrook's community leaders had a notion of what a complete community should look like. There was a hope to have available all of the amenities and advantages of bigger cities. There was an interest in building up the economic, educational, civic, and community foundations to enable the places called home to thrive. As it turns out, in many such places, the development of a YMCA was an acceptable, even compelling goal.

It did not hurt that so many men and women at the heart of community building had their own YMCA stories which connected them in a very strong way to the YMCA. Wherever they lived, it was not unusual to see them engage with the leadership advocating building new YMCAs. Sometimes this effort added a branch operation to a preexisting YMCA. Sometimes it led to building an independent association out of the fertile ground of civic activism. People seemed to want to live in a place that had a YMCA. This was, and is, good news for the YMCA and for the members benefitted by their association.

Ken Thiel was able to construct a small movement around the effort to build a new YMCA. The biggest challenge was raising the money to permanently plant the YMCA on the North Shore.

Two Gifts Make The Difference

There were a number of obstacles to realizing the dream of building a permanent and modern YMCA in Northbrook. Despite the fertile ground provided by the contemporary development of Northbrook's community life, a building campaign would be challenging.

Among the obstacles was the lack of community experience with what then would have been a major capital campaign. The community's only real experience with such efforts had been the various campaigns mounted to build and furnish facilities for religious congregations. These, however, were different from a prospective YMCA campaign. YMCA membership was still relatively small, in part because of the lack of a permanent programmed facility. The size of the campaign would be unprecedented in Northbrook. There was no availability of denominational support either for capital gifts, or for favorable financing tools, as was the case with most religious congregations. It had also been a long time since a new and independent YMCA was established in the Chicago suburbs, especially one not chartered as part of the great YMCA of Chicago

As it turned out, two significant and early gifts provided the leverage, endorsement, and encouragement needed for the campaign to build the North Suburban YMCA. These gifts were critical and transformative. They made it possible for the campaign to get off the ground and fly to a successful conclusion. The two entities that made that difference were the Allstate Insurance Company and the Swedish Covenant Church. It is interesting to recognize that these were, as previously noted, two of the newest actors on the business and civic scene when the YMCA was starting up in Northbrook.

Their two gifts made a hybrid gift in excess of a million dollars, each gift encouraging, challenging, and affirming the gift of the other. Each gift was part of the other. Neither was possible without the other and both made success almost assured. One gift was a pledge of direct cash support, the other a genuine in-kind gift of real substance. The cash gift paid for the keystone facility amenity anchoring the Y building: a beautiful state-of-the-art indoor Olympic-sized swimming pool. The other provided for an open-ended use of ten acres ceded to the Y for the building site of the new association for the duration of its history.

My own million-dollar moment was as part of the solicitation team for both of these gifts. I had prepped for solicitation visits with Ken. I gained exposure visiting various Rotary and other civic clubs. The Allstate and Covenant Church visits came to mean even more.

The Allstate gift for the first capital campaign represented the beginning of a relationship that has sustained itself over the intervening decades, sometimes with gaps, but sustained, none the less. There has usually been an Allstate director or officer on the Y's Board of Directors. Many Allstate employee families have been active at the Y. The latest large gift from Allstate to the Y came in the last few years as part of a YMCA debt reduction campaign. The company's giving to the YMCA has been important and strategic and has had sustained impact.

From the early 1950s forward, Allstate has built a robust corporate responsibility and philanthropic grants program. With over $400 million in gifts to charitable sector organizations since 1952, the company's giving now annually exceeds $30 million. Allstate has also engaged in a series of community building efforts focused on a range of issues. Current commitments include emphases on domestic violence, youth empowerment, and teen safe driving.

The Covenant Church gift had a unique and creative structure, as it represented a more or less permanent grant of access and utilization for the YMCA on ground owned by the church and retirement facility. This grant saved the Y hundreds of thousands of dollars, positioned it in a prime location, offered expansion space, and provided a partner with resources and integrity. One great boon to the Y was the development of a shared parking lot, so important in a car-based, suburban community.

The church grant was relatively unique for its day. Much of the North Suburban YMCA's work was also unique. In decades to come, similar deals would benefit YMCAs throughout the country. Today, one can find evidence of YMCA tenancy deals involving hospitals, schools, park districts, colleges, and other community organizations. There have even been a few agreements with large business enterprises.

When I was asked to be a spokesperson for the campaign, Ken challenged me to be very well-prepared, to use my own voice, and to be ready to speak to a diverse group of possible donors. Granting me good freedom, he nonetheless made sure that my message was crafted so that it fit with the YMCA "hymn book." I remember practicing with him, responding to his suggestions, and really studying and preparing with the campaign materials so expertly developed for the effort.

In this work, I learned to take cues from the voices and dialogue of adult volunteers and other professional staff members. I learned that the personal story was not only welcome but necessary when making a powerful case. I learned that some adults were truly interested in hearing young people. I learned to be grateful for the opportunity so generously extended to me to help write the future of my own community. I learned to love the YMCA even more than I did.

Leadership of both giving organizations was present in the campaign structure. Not satisfied in simply securing the blessing of institutional support from one's own organization, leaders at Allstate and at the Church also made personal gifts within the limits of their capabilities. These gifts were a personal statement of support, which further affirmed the campaign goals for the broader community.

In the midst of all of this, I came to know that my own parents were also pledging some of their modest income to support the new YMCA. Part of this commitment was a statement of loyalty and friendship to their neighbor Ken Thiel, the other was an affirmation of the observable impact of the Y on their two children. As it turns out, their gift was probably the largest capital campaign commitment they ever made. This, too, gave me encouragement and a certain pride to be a participant in the campaign. To this day, it gives me a genuine sense of happiness and connection to see their names on the "Builders Wall" at the YMCA.

I was not even then unaware of the extensive preparation, dialogue, and spadework required to bring most major solicited gifts to fruition. Mr. Thiel had been a reasonably successful tutor. It was clear to me that my youthful participation, though welcome, was part of a larger, more sustained effort. I came to know that I was more a part of the final scene in the last act of an engaging work of art that brought cause and donor together for the genuine affirmation of both. This was an enlightening and encouraging revelation.

When the North Suburban YMCA opened its doors to its new home on March 19, 1969, there was a genuine sense of accomplishment and excitement in the community. For its time, this new YMCA drew a lot of positive commentary. Its modern structure, its beneficial location, its community support group, and its business plan all brought positive attention inside and outside the YMCA movement.

In the next three decades, this small suburban YMCA would become a trendsetter in various YMCA practices. Some of its programs would lead the field in various areas. Ken's leadership would be sustained through his retirement.

Following Ken's retirement, the Y entered a period of challenge and decline. This experience reflected poor leadership choices, changing economic performance, and lack of innovation and initiative. By 2005, this once-shining exemplar of the independent YMCA was in debt, threatened with closure by the national YMCA, and a bit at sea in its own community.

Then a wonderful thing happened. With some significant support from the national YMCA, and a renewal of volunteer spirit, some time was bought to see if the Y could be saved. A new professional leader was engaged whose prior experience had been as an executive in the Jewish Community Center movement.

Howard Schultz was hired to be the Y's new CEO. He remains in his post after a bit more than ten years of service. He has led a revitalization of the North Suburban YMCA. The Y has recovered financially, invested heavily in modernization, positioned itself as an essential community partner, and built more community ties than ever before. Howard and his team are sure to experience their own million-dollar moments.

It is encouraging to know that a rebirth and renaissance is possible for challenged community organizations when they reassert their presence and purpose. Usually, this good work also dictates a reinvestment in a robust plan for philanthropic development.

Conclusion

It would have been impossible to guess where the career of a sixteen-year-old YMCA volunteer spokesman would take him. Even so, one pattern seemed to have been set in the late 1960s. Perhaps that pattern was laid out in the experience of that early million-dollar moment. If not destiny, perhaps fate or fortune has been at work.

In some form or fashion, I have been engaged in fundraising, philanthropy, and public advocacy for 50 years. This pattern has held true in high school, college, graduate school, career, and volunteer posts. It has worked its way into every career experience. It has even been a part of choices that brought me to the professional leadership of the YMCA of the USA in the first decade of the 21st Century in a very challenging time of change. It has even been an important part of early retirement from leadership in healthcare philanthropy in Texas.

The choice of illustrating my own million-dollar moment in the manner described above was motivated by an effort to dig into the roots of my own youthful experience. I wanted to see if some useful lessons could be divined from such exploration. At the end, I am not so sure, in part because it is hard to draw general conclusions from such individual and distinctive autobiography. All of us are so unique. Nonetheless, I hazard to express at least five lessons that seem apparent to me:

1. Philanthropy is transformative in the lives of individuals, institutions, and communities because, at its best, it puts mission first, and that mission is the improvement of the human condition in all its wonder and diversity.
2. Philanthropy is a team sport, and depends upon collective vision, cooperative work, and shared integrity. The ideal of trust lies very close to the heart of philanthropy.
3. Philanthropy should invite everyone to play their part, and everyone has something to contribute in the classic sharing of time, talent, and treasure. In this invitation, it is essential to include our children and youth if we are interested in building the future.
4. Philanthropy, at its best, works in the space of human relationships marked by the virtue of generosity. The practice of generosity is a discipline in every sense of the word. Generosity is key to the motivation of the donor. Activating that motivation is the core work of fundraising.
5. Philanthropy thrives where gratitude is expressed in both the giving and the receiving of gifts. The donor expresses gratitude by giving out of the abundance which is hers. The beneficiary responds in gratitude because he knows the gift is given with no thought of creating a debt.

I would like to believe that these lessons informed the effort to build the North Suburban YMCA in the 1960s. It is wonderful to believe so.

Admittedly, my million-dollar moment herein discussed is not one of the purest form. It was the result, as noted, of a hybrid gift. It was created by the combination of two donors' generosity. From a long career, I could have chosen any number of other purer examples. Yet, somehow, it made sense to me to choose this early YMCA experience. Perhaps it does to the reader, too. I certainly hope this is true! I started learning these lessons as a young man, and I am still learning.

About Kenneth L. Gladish, PhD

Gladish

Dr. Ken Gladish has been a leader in philanthropic and charitable organizations for more than 30 years.

Ken recently retired as President and CEO of the Seton Foundations. Seton is the largest nonprofit, charitable healthcare system in Central Texas. Its four fundraising foundations support its many ministries, projects and programs throughout Central Texas: Dell Children's Medical Center of Central Texas Foundation, Seton Hays Foundation, Seton Williamson Foundation and The Seton Fund.

Immediately prior to joining Seton, Ken served as President and CEO of the Austin Community Foundation.

Ken's distinguished career includes serving as President of the YMCA of the USA. Dr. Gladish began his career as the Assistant Director for Youth and Community Programs at the North Suburban YMCA outside of Chicago in the mid-1970s.

He joined the YMCA of the USA after serving six years as Executive Director of the Indianapolis Foundation and William E. English Foundation, and three years as President of the Central Indiana Community Foundation. Other leadership positions he held were President of the Indiana Humanities Council, Director of the Indiana Donors Alliance, and taught at Indiana University in Indianapolis and Butler University.

Dr. Gladish's also served as a Distinguished Professor of Nonprofit Studies and Director of the Grantmaking School at the Johnson Center for Philanthropy and Nonprofit Leadership in Grand Rapids, Michigan. His primary fields of teaching have been politics, leadership, philanthropic and nonprofit studies, and organizational management.

He has led organizations that have raised more than $600 million in charitable support, and has been intimately engaged in creating campaigns, seeding new initiatives and serving as a key resource in endowment, capital and annual support campaigns.

Ken holds a bachelor's degree in political science from Hanover College, and a master's and doctoral degrees in government and foreign affairs from the University of Virginia. And, he has been bestowed with three honorary doctoral degrees.

Family is extremely important to Ken. He is married to Kendal Gladish, also a graduate of Hanover College. Kendal is a communications consultant. They are the parents of Ellen and Donald.

CHAPTER FOURTEEN
Tom Smith and the Butler Way
By D. Mark Helmus

I arrived on the Butler University campus in the fall of 2003 after a rewarding four years at Franklin College where I was Executive Director of Development. A change in presidents at Franklin allowed me to pursue my interest in gift planning. I made the choice of Butler over Florida State University. As it turned out, I made an excellent decision. Butler would be my home for more than nine years, first as Senior Director of Development, Gift Planning, and later as Vice President for University Advancement. I would not have left Butler if my college fraternity, Delta Tau Delta, had not asked me to become its Executive Vice President for the Delta Tau Delta Educational Foundation.

In addition to the job responsibilities I would have, Butler offered another attraction for me personally and professionally. It was called "The Butler Way." It permeated throughout campus in its students, sports teams, alumni, and throughout the greater Indianapolis community. As articulated on the school's website, the Butler Way, "demands commitment, denies selfishness, accepts reality, yet seeks improvement every day while putting the team above self." These were values I sought to model as a husband, father, community member, and leader in my chosen profession.

While I had been involved with a few million-dollar gifts earlier in my career, the focus of this story came in my tenure at Butler University in 2006. I called on an alumnus, Tom Smith, who had graduated in the late 1940s after serving in World War II. He had been a regular donor, and had even established a charitable gift annuity or two over the years. I had no idea that this man who possessed a great smile and was devoid of ego would become an important part of my life over the next six years.

One of the university's greatest needs at this time was scholarships. Financial aid for its students was already a strength at Butler, but long-range plans called for a solid addition to what was already there.

Tuition at Butler in 2003 was $20,190 annually, not including the substantial costs for room and board, books, and fees. The University Advancement staff developed a number of naming opportunities for scholarships, and I found that our President, Dr. Bobby Fong, was a strong and willing advocate on behalf of the scholarship effort. As Dr. Fong told our students, "Discover your gifts, pursue your passions, and never forget that your own flourishing is always tied to promoting the well-being of others."[8] Scholarships helped provide students with the opportunity to attend Butler University and with the grounding to promote the well-being of others. It was our hope that scholarships would be appealing to Tom.

In preparing for our initial meeting, I discovered Tom thought the world of his wife (they were Butler classmates). I also learned he had his fingers in a number of different business items and was quite an entrepreneur. While at Butler, Tom was a member of Sigma Nu Fraternity. After his wife, Martha, his second love was his motorcycle. He took great pleasure in driving it around campus.

Interestingly enough, both Tom and I were influenced by Dick Skoolund. A member of the National Society of Fundraising Executives national board for four years, annual giving increased 650 percent at Butler under Dick's leadership. There was something about Dick that brought out the best in people. Perhaps it was his background as a minister who graduated from Northwest Christian College and Christian Theological Seminary before arriving at Butler. Dick had recruited me to Butler, and we were both members of St. Luke's United Methodist Church in Indianapolis. Dick had originally identified Tom as a donor prospect. Thanks to Dick's efforts, Tom had become a member of the Butler University planned giving society.

Tom and I first met at his home in East-Central Indiana. It was modest and well-maintained. I think part of the reason I hit it off so well with Tom was because, like Tom, I grew up in a small town, close to the shores of Lake Erie. There just seemed to be a natural bond.

His wife, Martha, had died in the preceding months, and it was clear he was still grieving and missed her very much. Martha, the daughter of a former United States Congressman, Albert R. Hall, was originally from Marian, Indiana, and majored in business administration at Butler. Like Tom, she was active on campus, including membership in Kappa Kappa Gamma sorority. Martha and Tom married in 1947, one year after graduation, and lived in Rush County for 56 years. Theirs was a true love story.

I learned early on that Tom had made his career in the insurance industry. As for hobbies, he enjoyed motorcycles in his younger days. He and his wife did not have children, though he had extended family and friends galore. He had great feelings for his alma mater and for his college fraternity, Sigma Nu.

During our meeting, Tom mentioned several "properties" he wanted to discuss gifting. He described them as small, commercial structures in nearby Indiana communities. Tom estimated the total value to be "maybe a couple-hundred thousand, but probably less than that." I thanked him for his interest in considering such a gift, and went about arranging to see the properties with him. After that second visit, I agreed to recommend that Butler accept the properties, although knowing his initial estimated value was probably high.

Following our tour, while talking over lunch, he shared with me a little about his father. He recalled driving cross-country from Indiana to the Los Angeles area. I asked him about the purpose of the trip, and he said it was to visit his dad's "investment interests" there. With curiosity raised, discussion ensued which ultimately led to his multi-million-dollar gift. It turns out that his dad owned two eight-unit apartment complexes in a comfortable area of Los Angles. When his father died, Tom received the properties through the estate. He had not been to visit them in person for more than 40 years. When we dug in to how much he was paying for property management and oversight, it was clear he was not keeping the properties to increase his wealth. Quite the contrary, as my suspicion was that he was being taken advantage of, which I think he knew to be the case, too.

Because Tom associated those properties so closely to his father, he couldn't bring himself to sell or gift them during his life. However, he did adjust his estate plans to gift the properties to Butler upon his death, which unfortunately occurred shortly thereafter. Sale of these properties netted $2.2 million. The funds established endowed scholarships in his and his wife's names. Due to Tom's philanthropy, the impact upon Butler University students interested in business careers will be felt for many years to come.

An official citation at Butler University reads:

"The Martha H. and W. Thomas Smith Scholarship was established through a generous estate gift by Martha and Thomas Smith, both graduates of Butler's Class of 1946. Active in the Butler community during their collegiate years, the Smiths remained connected to Butler throughout their lives. The couple were married in 1947, and were active in the Rushville, Indiana, community where they made their home. The scholarship is awarded to students pursuing a degree in the Lacy School of Business."

During my fundraising tenure, before and after Butler University, I have met many loyal and generous donors. Few, however, showed Tom's humility, sense of humor, and love for family, friends and the organizations that were most were important to him.

I learned so much over the years from Tom Smith, a very unique and unassuming individual. He embodied the true meaning of being philanthropic. Tom helped make me a much better resource development professional in several ways:

- Stewardship—Working with Tom helped me see a broad range of possibilities for helping students through philanthropy.
- Cooperation and Teamwork—Coordinating with Dick Skooglund, Bobby Fong, University Advancement staff, and our board made this million-dollar moment a reality. In addition, I reached out to other professionals in real estate and finance in east central Indiana and Los Angeles, people I had never met before. Without their assistance, Tom's gift would not have been possible.

- Personal Enjoyment—Gratifying to me as a resource development professional is getting to know donors as people, too. These are bonds and memories which last a lifetime, while enhancing the organization's mission.

I will always have a warm spot in my heart for Tom Smith.

About D. Mark Helmus

Helmus

D. Mark Helmus has served as the Senior Vice President for Development for the Ball State University Foundation (BSUF) since August, 2015. He, along with the BSUF President and CEO, Executive Vice President, and Vice President for Strategic Engagement and Communication, comprise the Foundation's Executive Leadership Team.

Mark leads the BSUF Development Team of 25 employees focused on capital campaigns, major gifts, planned gifts, foundation relations, athletics development, and prospect research. Plans are underway for a fundraising initiative in conjunction with the University's centennial in 2018-19, and a larger comprehensive campaign for Ball State's second century of education, leadership, and service.

Prior to Ball State, he served as the Executive Vice President of the Delta Tau Delta Educational Foundation. During his tenure, his second with the organization, the Foundation set records for total fundraising and made strategic decisions to maximize resources on pipeline development, increase personalized prospect engagement, discontinue a waning telemarketing program, and challenge the ROI of owning the organization's headquarters.

Mark spent the prior nine years at Butler University, the first three as Senior Director of Gift Planning, and then, the remainder as Vice President of University Advancement. During his tenure, the University raised over $163 million in total cash, averaging more than $18 million per year, and successfully concluded the ButlerRising comprehensive capital campaign, exceeding its $125 million goal by nearly $30 million. His leadership helped Butler have its top three fundraising years, while moving into the Top-20 Master's Comprehensive Universities and Colleges based on alumni giving rate (20th out of 576 in 2010).

Other professional experiences included Franklin College as Interim Vice President for Advancement and the Executive Director of Development, the Milton and Rose D. Friedman Foundation, the Ruth Lilly Health Education Center, Ruotolo Associates (campaign counsel), and the Delta Tau Delta Educational Foundation. Before entering the fundraising field in 1991, he served Delta Tau Delta Fraternity as a chapter consultant and the University of Tennessee, Knoxville as its Advisor for Fraternities.

Mark earned his bachelor's degree in psychology from Ohio University and a master's degree in higher education administration from the University of Tennessee. He currently serves on the Board of Directors and is the immediate past chairman of Starfish Initiative, a not-for-profit college-access mentoring program, is a past president of the Planned Giving Group of Indiana (PGGI), and former chair of the St. Luke's United Methodist Church Endowment Committee.

Mark met his wife, Carol, in 1991 through their work as Greek fundraisers. Carol is an executive for Delta Delta Delta Educational Foundation. She is a three-term member of the Lawrence Township School Board. They have two children, Jacob, a rising senior at Indiana University, and Caitlin, who also attends Indiana University as a freshman.

CHAPTER FIFTEEN

The Legacy of Stella and Charles Guttman

By Scott E. Evenbeck, PhD

Every major philanthropic gift has important and multi-layered stories that accompany it. What triggered the donation, what problem will be addressed, and what sort of impact the gift will have are the stories communicated to the public at large when the gift is first announced. However, the private and semi-public discussions that precede any large gift have the potential to lend the donation even more power if the timing and the people are right. The story behind the gift that established the endowment at my college is such a story.

In early 2008, Matthew Goldstein, Chancellor of the City University of New York (CUNY), commissioned faculty, staff, and administrators across CUNY to work with national leaders in undergraduate education to design a new model for a community college. One singularly focused on enhancing student success and drawing on the latest research and best practices associated with student success. The school would be the first new community college opened by CUNY in over four decades. Goldstein's charge was bold: reimagine the delivery of a community college education that would result in higher retention rates and quicker degree completion.

CUNY's John Mogulescu, Senior University Dean for Academic Affairs, and his colleagues, with the support of the Bill and Melinda Gates Foundation and other significant resources from CUNY, developed a concept paper for the new college. Tracy Meade of CUNY headed the implementation team for development of the college. Gussie Kappner, who had served as President of the Borough of Manhattan Community College and of Bank Street College of Education, led the search for the founding President of what was then called the "New Community College."

There was a precedent for what Goldstein and CUNY wanted to achieve, set at University College of Indiana University-Purdue University Indianapolis (IUPUI). Jerry Bepko, Chancellor of IUPUI, and Bill Plater, Dean of Faculties at IUPUI, had worked with an IUPUI team at a summer institute of the Association of American Colleges and Universities (AAC&U) to confront IUPUI's unacceptable outcomes with its entering students. Bepko, Plater, and their team proposed a new school for the IUPUI campus, called the University College, and spent a year working with faculty and administrative leaders on the project. The Faculty Council overwhelmingly approved the new unit, and I was named Dean.

The faculty of University College, drawn from all the other schools at IUPUI, developed programs and practices to enhance student academic achievement and persistence. This effort moved forward during the administration of Miles Brand, President of Indiana University, whose leadership resulted in a significant Retention Grant from The Lilly Endowment. I was the co-leader of that effort, and it moved forward through Brand's strategic investment of university resources and IUPUI's commitment of campus resources. A team of faculty leaders from IUPUI's School of Liberal Arts, working with Associate Dean Barbara Jackson and Assistant Dean Gayle Williams, also appointed to work with this new academic unit, spent a year designing and implementing means for IUPUI's entering students to join the scholarly community in a uniquely supportive and challenging environment.

The first decade of University College saw significant increases in the retention and graduation rates for IUPUI's students. A Council on Retention and Graduation, which I chaired, took center stage in overseeing campus attention to student success, centered in University College, but engaging all of IUPUI's schools and key administrative units. IUPUI was engaged in the first cohort of Foundations of Excellence colleges in the seminal work of John Gardner and Betsy Barefoot on enhancing student success. IUPUI was also one of the ten universities participating in the AAC&U's Greater Expectations project. Working across institutions, IUPUI faculty and staff learned from these knowledgeable friends and formed communities of practice centered on student academic achievement and persistence. Support from the Pew Charitable Trusts enabled IUPUI to collaborate with

Temple University and Portland State University in the "Restructuring for Urban Student Success" project with Nancy Hoffman, a long-time leader in educational innovation, as the coordinator of the multi-year collaboration. IUPUI sought out best practices and implemented learning communities, coordinated programs of study for first-year students, very much influenced by faculty visits to CUNY's LaGuardia Community College, and also a summer bridge program, a function of a Federal Fund for the Improvement of Postsecondary Education (FIPSE) grant to CUNY's Brooklyn College, with founder Martha Bell.

The work at IUPUI, LaGuardia Community College, and Brooklyn College informed the planning and program building for the New Community College. For example, the planned program sought to replicate IUPUI's Bridge Program, which was modelled on the program at Brooklyn College. However, we have learned that there is a vast difference between starting a program and developing a new college. Since I was serving as the Founding Dean of University College at IUPUI, Kappner and her colleagues recruited me to apply for the position of founding President. I was appointed at the July 2010 meeting of the CUNY Board of Trustees.

The first faculty for the New Community College began their work in September 2010, and I joined the effort in January 2011. The subsequent 18 to 24 months were hectic and hard. Hiring, curriculum development, admissions outreach and building preparations (the new College is still in a rented building) happened simultaneously. The first students started their Bridge Program on August 20, 2012, a day marked by New York's Mayor Michael Bloomberg and Chancellor Goldstein celebrating the formation of the new college at the opening convocation at the New York Public Library.

Meanwhile, just a few city blocks away, the Stella and Charles Guttman Foundation was seeking means for maintaining and preserving the legacy of its founders, Stella and Charles Guttman. Charles was born on Manhattan's Lower East Side of an immigrant family. From his father, Adolph, a Romanian emigre, Charles learned an appreciation for education, a respect for hard work, a belief in the equality of opportunity for all people, and a firm commitment to helping those in need. The Foundation reported the following in a celebratory brochure, published on the 35th anniversary of the Foundation's founding:

Charles, the second of Adolph's four children, was born in September 1892. He attended Public School 20 and was graduated before he was 13, when his formal education came to an end. As a child, Charles was enormously resourceful, taking odd jobs to earn his way. He made a nickel for each message he delivered for the New York Stock Exchange. When immigrants arrived at Ellis Island, he earned 20 cents for escorting them to their relatives' homes.

Charles suffered from the problems of growing up in the densely populated, difficult living conditions of the Lower East Side. His own experience with youthful delinquent behavior led to his commitment as an adult to help children overcome the problems they face in our society.

In 1937, Charles founded The Paddington Corporation, which became the exclusive importer of Justerini and Brooks Ltd. (J&B), a creator of fine wines and whiskies.

In November 1959, Charles Guttman, with his wife, Stella Rappaport Guttman, founded the Guttman Foundation to continue the family's charitable tradition. The Foundation's purpose was broadly described as the "improvement and benefit of mankind, and the alleviation of human suffering." Upon their deaths in 1969, the Guttmans bequeathed substantially all of their assets to the Foundation.

The philanthropic legacy of Stella and Charles Guttman remains the guiding principle of the Foundation's Board, which includes third generation family members.

After the Foundation passed its 50th anniversary, the Board addressed the issue of the Foundation's future. The Board had shrunk to five members, three of whom were in or close to their 80s. The future governance and administration of the Foundation was a major concern. A proposal was made to find a major institution likely to survive indefinitely and transfer the Foundation's entire assets (then over $50 million) to an endowment that would preserve in perpetuity the Guttman name and legacy.

While this proposal was not acceptable to a majority of the Board, the Foundation did begin a strategic review with the aid of an outside consulting firm. All of the Board members were actively involved in this process. After this study, the Board voted to spend half its assets on no more than two major projects. The Board gave higher education the top priority and eventually decided to devote $25 million to that cause. The directors later added five members to the Board, each with extensive experience and expertise in the nonprofit world.

Elizabeth Olofson, executive director of the Guttman Foundation, was charged by the Board to investigate CUNY as a possible partner in extending the Guttman legacy to serve underserved children and youth in New York City. Jessica Chou, who served as an advisor to the Foundation, recommended that Elizabeth visit the New Community College. Elizabeth then arranged for all the board members to visit the college and learn about its commitment to student success. Carlos Flynn and Duffie Cohen of CUNY's Central Office Advancement Staff joined the conversations with the Guttman Foundation.

These conversations and investigations resulted in the Foundation making an investment of $25 million in CUNY's community colleges, with $15 million earmarked as an endowed student success fund for the new community college. Another $9 million was placed in a transfer scholarship endowment to give scholarships to top-performing students at CUNY's seven community colleges to help them continue their educations at one of CUNY's five senior colleges. An additional $1 million was earmarked for current use to CUNY's Accelerated Study in the Associate Programs (ASAP) initiative. Chancellor Goldstein, working with then-Chair Benno Schmidt and other members of CUNY's Board, determined it appropriate to memorialize this gift, then the largest ever to a community college, with the renaming of the community college as the Stella and Charles Guttman Community College.

At the CUNY Board of Trustees meeting on April 29, 2013, when the Board approved the gift and renamed the College, Guttman Foundation President Ernest Rubenstein made the following remarks:

"I would like to start by thanking Executive Director Olofson who spent two years leading the due diligence effort, interviewing just about every organization that deals with college education in the City of New York—everyone that tries to help poor kids get into, remain and succeed at college. She has done a fantastic job. When I first thought of devoting a good part of the Foundation's endowment, I was looking at the extreme right end of the bell curve to try to find those poor kids who had enormous talent and whose careers should be subsidized. The more we studied this, the more I realized those kids are going to get into the top colleges anyway. There is loads of money available for their scholarships. I started to worry about the kids at the other end of the bell curve. Then I heard a speech at the New York Historical Society by Neil Ferguson last year, the noted historian now at Harvard, and someone asked him if he was concerned about the enormous disparities of wealth in this country—a disparity getting worse and not better. He responded that does not worry him as much as the need to insure that the ladder or escalator for social and economic elevation remains available to poor kids: That is what is important, because if you do not have that, then you are sowing the seeds of a society that will be less stable in future years. This is terribly important to me because if the Guttmans were alive, they would be delighted as they did not have any children and I always felt that the Foundation was their DNA and it was our obligation to preserve their name associated with good deeds. CUNY will be around 50 and 100 years from now as will its colleges and it will continue to carry the Guttman name. So on the theory that it is better to give than to receive, Executive Director Olofson and I are content and delighted to be here. I am so happy that you found this proposal acceptable."

The Student Success Fund has been transformative for the college and its students. The Fund supports a wide array of experiential education programs for the college, for example, making it possible for students to study abroad and to conduct undergraduate research. Since 2014, teams of Guttman students, working with faculty, have done research in Germany, Alaska, Jamaica, El Salvador, Ecuador, Belize, and Chile. The students design their own research projects ranging from conservation studies to research on rare species to the social and economic impact of tourism-based economies and to public health and urban social and cultural issues. It is not an overstatement to say that the College uses its endowment funds to connect the students in dynamic ways to the world around them, not as passive recipients of social services or knowledge but as active agents of change.

In his remarks to the CUNY Board, Rubenstein talked about how he hoped the Guttman students would live out the DNA coming with the legacy of Stella and Charles Guttman. These students would be the children the Guttmans never had. It is the aspiration of the college to live out that legacy, and the trustees of the Guttman Foundation sense and greatly appreciate the college's respect for and dedication to the Guttmans. There is a remarkable match in the foundation's vision for the use of their grant and the college's work with students. Foundation board members have retained a keen interest in the welfare and work of the college, regularly attending student presentations, convocations, and commencements.

The story of Charles, the gift itself, and the creation of the college have blended together into a narrative that lends energy and transformative power to the students. Ramon Mendez, a 2015 graduate of Guttman and a 2017 graduate of CUNY's famed City College, gave the Alumni Greeting at the Guttman College's 2017 Fourth Annual Commencement in June 2017. In these excerpts of his speech, you can see how this remarkable young man respects the power of personal struggle and transformation:

> "Each one of us has had a different journey to how we have come to this commencement today. For many of us that journey includes coming to this country. As a man, a person of color, a child of undocumented parents, an immigrant, a first-

generation college student, many people might not expect that I would be here today talking to you, my future fellow alumni. Whatever label might apply to you, we share a bond. That bond is that we have all attempted and now are succeeding in obtaining a college degree…

It might seem like just yesterday you were walking into Guttman for Summer Bridge, maybe at some point you wondered how you were going to be stuck with the same cohort for an entire year. Love it or hate it, your cohort became your peers and, in many cases, your friends. To this day I am friends with some of my cohort, House 3 Cohort 3 from 2013…

How many of you are also thinking about members of your cohort who haven't made it here today? Some of them surely will graduate next year—but others perhaps are no longer students at Guttman. What happened to them? Why aren't they here? I ask you to reflect on them, and don't forget them. While you remember them, value your own accomplishments all the more.

Many of us know how hard it is to live as people of color and as immigrants in the current political climate. So take a look around you and pat yourself on the back. You have proven many around this country wrong and maybe even some in this very room wrong. But what is more or equally important is that you have also proven to yourself that you are capable of doing anything you put your mind to.

Now I will tell you something about my experience at City College, and that is Guttman was way more difficult! Guttman challenged me to think beyond the mere memorization of facts.

At Guttman I learned how to be a critical thinker, which has allowed me to make the connections between what I learned in the classroom and what I learned in my everyday life.

Another valuable lesson I learned at Guttman is how

important it is for us to take care of ourselves, to not burn out, to not stretch ourselves too thin—because the world needs us—you—to right wrongs, to go out there and fight for what we know is right.

So when you go to your senior colleges or your jobs—remember this—You Need to Take Care of Yourself. Don't be afraid, the lessons you learned at Guttman have put you ahead of the game. You might not believe this—you might be a little scared—but have confidence. Remember how you felt at the start of Bridge?—and here you are—sitting at your Commencement! You got this.

Between the long papers and all the Community Days, the surveys, the labs, the studios, the GLOs [Guttman Learning Outcomes] and the enforced touch points—you did it! Congratulations, and continue to prove any naysayers wrong.

Had Charles and Stella Guttman had the opportunity to hear Ramon's speech, I like to think they would have been very, very proud.

There are a number of lessons one can draw from this experience, including: core values and vision are imperative; the funder has to be clear in its aspirations; the recipient has to be very clear in its purposes and mission; and when an ongoing relationship is possible, that is a good thing.

This story has a particularly happy ending: in August 2016, as Guttman College was preparing for its fifth year, the National Center for Education Statistics' College Navigator named Guttman Community College as the best Community College in the State of New York.

About Scott E. Evenbeck, PhD

Evenbeck

Scott Evenbeck was named Guttman Community College's Founding President in 2011. Guttman Community College opened its doors in 2012. During the last five years, its academic program has been very successful, with graduation rates exceeding the national average almost three-fold. Guttman Community College was among eleven institutions selected by Diverse: Issues In Higher Education as the 2017 Most Promising Places to Work in Community Colleges.

Dr. Evenbeck is a member of the Presidents' Alliance on Higher Education and Immigration which is comprised of over two dozen distinguished leaders of public and private universities and university systems, liberal arts colleges, and community colleges, representing hundreds of thousands of students, faculty, and staff from institutions across the United States.

Previously, Scott served as Professor of Psychology, Associate Vice Chancellor for Undergraduate Education, and Founding Dean of University College at Indiana University-Purdue University Indianapolis (IUPUI).

Long involved in designing, implementing and assessing first-year experience programs for students, he has given more than 100 presentations at academic conferences, and he has written many articles and chapters on academic achievement and persistence.

Scott was a task force advisor for the Foundations of Excellence in the First College Year, the Building Engagement and Attainment for Minority Students (BEAMS) project of the Institute for Education Policy (IHEP), the Learning Communities Institute of the Washington Center for Undergraduate Education, and the General Education and Assessment Institute of the Association of American Colleges and Universities, and he served on accrediting teams for three regional accrediting bodies.

Other service includes the Board of the American Conference of Academic Deans, the John N. Gardner Institute for Excellence in Undergraduate Education, and other national associations.

Scott is a native of Fostoria, Ohio. He holds a bachelors degree from Indiana University, and master's and doctoral degrees from the University of North Carolina. Scott is the father of Ben and has a lovely granddaughter.

CHAPTER SIXTEEN
I Still Have The Voicemail On My Phone
By Sharon Pierce

Oh, that alarm clock went off so early on Saturday mornings. My twin brothers and I were still teenagers and my youngest brother, Randy, was only ten. Weren't kids our age supposed to sleep until noon on the weekends?

Not according to my dad. Ever since my mother's diagnosis of breast and then ovarian cancer at the age of 41, my father was on a mission to teach us that God calls us to love one another. Through his strong, compassionate example, he was guiding his four children to change our priorities from focusing on ourselves, to focusing on others. I was blessed to grow up in a Christian family where God's gifts of love, grace, and faith were evident.

As a child, I was the typical girl next door. Chipmunk cheeks, thunder thighs, a constant smile, and a love for and faith in people—children, adults, the elderly. I even liked the principals of my schools. My favorite school activity? Cheerleading!

Sunday School and church were a regular ritual in our family's life. Mother taught the three-year-old Sunday School class, for years and my father sang in the choir when he wasn't dozing. My twin brothers were 18 months younger than I was and were the largest twins ever born in Indiana. My brother, Randy, was nine years my junior, and he had those gorgeous long eyelashes and curly hair that Mom would have loved her only daughter to have. We had very limited financial resources, but we were blessed with a strong, Christian family, healthy bodies, and a love for each other, school and life in general.

Our family was very open about sharing our love and faith with others. That was probably why I have always been drawn to social work. My mother and grandmother were selfless in their daily examples of servant leadership, always doing whatever they could to help someone in need. Serving others was an integral part of my life as a child and as a teenager, but a series of life-changing events led to a sudden reordering of priorities for me and my family, clearly driven by what we thought God wanted from us.

When I was in high school, my mother was diagnosed with breast cancer, a rarity in those days and at a time when there were no support groups, no pink ribbons, and no understanding. My family and I were on that roller-coaster ride of emotions that faces every family touched by cancer. We prayed that the lump would not be malignant, but it was. We prayed that the radiation and chemotherapy would not cause the severe reactions in her that it had in others, but of course, it did.

Everyone around us shared our shock and despair. "Why Eileen Smith," they all asked. She was the mother of four children, a devoted wife, a strong Christian, President of the PTA, a loyal friend. Her body, spirit, and soul were brave, but her heart was broken. The friends to whom she had been so loyal and loving had abandoned her. The same friends whom she had served in every possible way would see me at the store doing our grocery shopping and run the other way, for they didn't know what to say.

One of the most poignant and painful memories I recall was when Mom yanked off her wig in front of the large dining room mirror looking at her bald head and screaming "Is this why my friends don't want to see me?!" We fell into each other's arms sobbing. I vowed and promised that no friend of mine, no loved one, no family member, would ever feel as lonely and unloved in their time of need as my mother was feeling. I was going to make certain that my life would be one where I would live my faith and spend my time serving others.

Despite challenges at home, I graduated from high school with honors. I wanted so much to go to Wittenberg University, but the distance and the cost were prohibitive with Mom's health. So, I decided on Ball State University, which I'm sure was God's plan because that is where I met my wonderful husband, Steve, and many lifelong friends.

During my college years, Mom's cancer recurred in the form of ovarian cancer. The long and painful years of battling this aggressive cancer were filled with major medical misdiagnoses. Mother defied all the odds and lived to see my youngest brother graduate from high school. At the age of 48, her seven-year struggle was over and the peace that she so deserved came at last.

What about those early Saturday mornings? As the first non-doctor ever elected president of the local cancer society, dad bought an old, black Ford truck—even though we couldn't afford it—and my brothers and I helped haul wigs, hospital beds, and comfortable chairs from one end of Fort Wayne, Indiana to the other. We were embarrassed to death of that old truck, but we were learning firsthand how to serve others, and we were blessed to have our father as a great example.

Barely six months after mother died, I got a phone call from a doctor friend of ours who had worked closely with dad on the Cancer Society's Board. "I don't know how to tell you this, Sharon," he began, "but your father has throat cancer." I couldn't believe it.

Dad's healthy roots as a "farm boy" helped him battle his cancer for over fifteen years. Because the surgical procedures used on him were so innovative, Dad's mission became helping others to benefit from research on his case.

In the midst of this challenge, Steve and I learned we were expecting our first child, just as we'd hoped and planned, three years after our marriage. Like any young couple, we were thrilled. This little gift from God surprised us one June morning by arriving three months early. The second surprise was that our first-born turned out to be identical twin girls. The doctor announced this possibility in the delivery room when he exclaimed, "Gee, this baby isn't even the size of a nice roast! I wonder if there's another one in here!" Courtney and Brittany hovered at two pounds each and spent their first three months in the intensive care nursery of Lutheran Hospital in Fort Wayne. Their birth became another faith-focusing experience for us. As they struggled to survive, the neonatal nurses marveled at how we were coping—so did we—and often asked us to counsel other parents of preemies, which we saw an opportunity to share our faith and hope with others. This further solidified my desire to make my own life's work serving others. Courtney and Brittany not only survived but they thrived, graduating from high school with 4.0-plus grade point averages, countless varsity letters in cross country, track, and cheerleading, and having the principal say he had never seen any students as kind to everyone as they were.

Following his first four surgeries, dad had a series of strokes, a broken hip, and a painful battle with adeno carcinoma, a cancer of the organs. This active, healthy farm boy weighed only 65 pounds when he died.

Both my father and my mother taught me as much about priorities, faith, and life in their dying as they did in their living. They never gave up hope, they never lost their dignity, and they never lost their love for us or their faith in their savior. Because they trusted in God's will themselves, they were able, always, to live out God's will in their lives.

On a crisp November day, my youngest brother, Randy, began having dizzy spells. Late one Sunday, he ended up in the emergency room where he subsequently had a brain scan. There was a large tumor encompassing the brain. Everyone was confident that this time our beloved family member would get the report "benign." How I wish I could say that that was the case, but the pathology reports indicated Randy had non-Hodgkin's lymphoma, a deadly brain cancer that was almost always fatal. His wife, Sandy, my brothers, our families and I attacked this shocking challenge with a vengeance, but there were no options. Randy's own spunky sense of humor became medicine for all of us. Randy died in early June, two days after his 43rd birthday, with all of us affirming and loving him those last difficult weeks. Our pastor reminded us at his beautiful funeral service that we might ask "why," but Randy never did.

How intriguing it is that some of life's most challenging experiences can fortify us, not only for our life's work, but for the privilege of serving others. Despite the traumatic losses of my beloved mother, father, and youngest brother, I was touched each and every day, by the foundation of faith, unconditional love and acceptance that I was blessed with throughout my childhood. I wanted that for every child in our neighborhoods and communities.

Following the surprise premature birth of our twins, Courtney and Brittany, Steve and I were blessed with a son, Brad, and a younger daughter, Ashley. We worked diligently to create the environment of unconditional love for our four amazing children that our own parents had created for us.

My venture into social work began in my hometown of Fort Wayne, when I worked with inner-city children on behalf of United Way. As my husband's career in agricultural business finance took us to Decatur and Champaign, Illinois, I was fortunate to experience additional great job opportunities, as well.

In Decatur, I was honored to serve as the Executive Director of Youth Advocate Program, an innovative nonprofit which was using volunteer advocates to mentor at-risk teenage youth. Often, my own children would get the chance to meet these vulnerable boys and girls. I loved that they realized they were no different than them or their friends, just a little older.

When we moved to the Champaign-Urbana area, I was named Regional Executive Director for the Children's Home and Aid Society of Illinois, a century-old statewide agency. I was responsible for the downstate child welfare programs for eight years, which was a great chance to broaden my skills and to become involved nationally with child welfare issues through Child Welfare League of America.

One of Children's Home and Aid's premier services was a runaway and homeless youth shelter, Round House, which served hundreds of vulnerable teens each year. I asked the staff to call me any time we had a young person who was having a birthday or deserved a special celebration; and the Pierce family station wagon would pick them up, take them to dinner, and give them a special gift. Courtney, Brittany, Brad, and Ashley quickly noticed how very grateful each teenager was for a small, random act of kindness. They each have huge hearts and demonstrate servant leadership, today, thanks to our shared exposure to those who simply don't have the blessing of a loving family and safe home. How grateful I am that the work I love has touched and changed their lives, too.

Our move back to Indiana in 1990 was a difficult one. Courtney and Brittany were high school freshmen, Brad was in middle school, and I had a job I loved. Ashley was young enough—a kindergartner—that she set the example for the rest of us by going with the flow. With

Steve's job moving to Indianapolis, it was a great opportunity for him, so we let our three oldest children decide where we were going to live by visiting several school districts. Zionsville was the winner, and we have loved our home, our church, and our community ever since.

Shortly after our move, I was fortunate enough to be presented with the opportunity to serve as the Deputy Director of the Indiana Division of Family and Children. It was a phenomenal, terrific learning experience. As the Director of Indiana Public Child Welfare System, I oversaw all 92 counties' child and family service programs, had the chance to work with other state agencies, learned more than I wanted to know about federal funding streams, and began to develop relationships with Indiana's legislators and policy makers.

I also worked with The Villages of Indiana's Board Officers on some challenging licensing regulations. They subsequently approached me about interviewing for the role of President and CEO, when their current leader, Dan Fulton, announced his retirement. I truly felt called to assume the exciting position, and it has been a labor of love for 25 years.

Every nonprofit leader works hand in hand, not only with their dedicated staff, but also with committed, volunteer board leaders. I have been privileged to have board of director chairs who share my passion for the mission and have brought unbelievable gifts to our organization and its growth. John Pless, as the Founder, in 1978, and initial board chairman of The Villages, had a vision of "Championing Families for Children" that still permeates every service and program of our statewide, $22 million life-changing nonprofit.

John Ackerman was the board chairman who helped us strategically create the Foundation, and served as the fund development arm of The Villages. Shokrina Radpour Beering guided our desire to become a member of the United Way of Central Indiana's family of agencies. Tim Franson and Kathi Postlethwait set the bar for engaging The Villages Board in "100-percent giving," a standard that has been in place for more than a decade.

David Barrett and Rhonda Yoder Breman provided steady hands and invaluable wisdom to shepherd The Villages through the most challenging chapter of our 40-year history, where unprecedented budget cuts occupied hundreds of hours of thoughtful deliberations.

As is often the case, nonprofit boards depend greatly on a few key leaders to instill that constantly-needed culture of generosity into the organization. The 3,000 abused, neglected, and vulnerable children that The Villages is privileged to serve each day have brighter futures thanks to Tim, Kathi, and Eileen Williams. This trio has been relentless in their quest to aggressively seek private donors and foundations who will enable The Villages to provide the quality services for which we are known, and that every child, youth and family touched by our work deserve.

Tim, Kathi, and Eileen crafted a pair of initiatives which have, since 2009, changed and stimulated the culture and the commitment of The Villages board of directors. It has ensured that our organization can always stand in the gap for the thousands of Indiana's abused, neglected, and abandoned children who need and deserve the same quality services and support that the children in our own lives have. Daily, we say we do not want to just serve children; we want to enrich their lives so they can achieve their full potential. That can only happen if The Villages can complement the very limited state and federal dollars received with adequate private contributions to assure quality.

Kathi served as Chairwoman of The Villages "A Place To Call Home" initiative, which raised $1 million dollars to help purchase what is now The Villages Child and Family Service Center at 3833 North Meridian Street in Indianapolis. It is a phenomenal office and program hub in the heart of the city, and close to where so many of the children and families we serve live.

Meanwhile, Tim and Eileen were immersed in providing leadership for the next effort. When The Villages Board of Directors held its Annual Board Retreat in 2014, Board Members unanimously agreed to be bold and embark on a $4 million human capital initiative, "Brighter Futures Are Within Our Reach," to invest in the people who are The Villages: the children, youth, families, foster parents, kinship caregivers, adoptive parents, and the tireless staff. The campaign explained exactly what the effort was about, creating brighter futures for the 11,000 individuals whose lives are touched by The Villages annually. With David Mills taking the mantle of leadership from Tim and Eileen, "Brighter Futures" will not only reach but exceed its $4 Million Goal.

It was through the "Brighter Futures Are Within Our Reach" initiative that The Villages received its first million-dollar gift.

A million dollars! How many times had I hoped and prayed for a million dollar gift? A gift large enough that we could provide even greater support for our more than 300 dedicated foster families. A gift that would allow us to assist additional heroic grandparents, who, with no notice whatsoever, are suddenly raising their grandchildren. A gift that would help parents who have huge hearts but aren't blessed with huge salaries, become a "forever family" and adopt a brother and sister in foster care who are yearning for a family of their own. A gift that would prevent child abuse and neglect from ever occurring by being able to serve even more first-time, at-risk parents with the national evidence-based Healthy Families Program.

Yes, I had contemplated the vital need for a formidable million-dollar gift; yet, I had never asked for a million dollars. That changed when The Villages board of directors and leadership team unanimously decided to be bold and embark on a private fundraising initiative, the "Brighter Futures" campaign, with a goal of raising $4 million.

The need for additional resources to supplement declining government funding had never been greater. Because of drastic reductions by the state in the reimbursement rates of foster care, adoption, and family services for private providers, child welfare agencies like The Villages simply couldn't continue to fulfill their mission without the infusion of private dollars. As we watched, nearly 30 of our peer agencies closed their doors and were forced to abandon their mission. Our resolve to succeed was cemented.

The faces and voices of The Villages' life-changing mission resonated with the generous individual donors and Foundation leaders. We made them aware of the harsh reality that children were the latest victims of Indiana's growing opioid and drug crisis. Donors responded with gifts and pledges that, when combined with 100-percent giving by

The Villages' Board of Directors, resulted in $1 million in donations, money that would be used to assist Indiana's most vulnerable children.

The strategic framework for The Villages' "Be Bold" initiative was aligning just as we had hoped. With $1 million already committed, I developed a proposal that would enable The Villages to continue to be industry leaders for Indiana's abused and neglected children. I then requested a meeting with David Biber, Secretary of Lilly Endowment, Inc., who oversaw all youth development requests.

Never had I been more nervous than I was prior to our meeting with David. The Lilly Endowment has been a generous, valued partner of The Villages of Indiana since our founding in 1978. Yet, I was requesting three times more than we had ever asked for in previous grants. As I shared the details of how we planned to use the funds, David simply said, calmly, "I think we can do this."

After conferring with Clay Robbins, CEO of Lilly Endowment, David called with the answer. I still have the voicemail in my phone, with David telling me that The Villages' $1 million grant request had been approved. It was the one day I truly wished I liked champagne, but I treated myself to a venti chai tea latte from Starbucks instead.

The Villages first million-dollar gift, and the dollars which matched it, have enabled us to meet unprecedented needs. We were able to recruit and train more foster families than ever before, secure an increased number of forever adoptive families for children whose parents have been lost to the tsunami of drug addiction, and continually grow the number of selfless grandparents who are reordering their lives to raise their grandchildren.

The gift from the Lilly Endowment has been truly transformational. After ten years of reduced reimbursement rates for our core child welfare services—foster care, adoption, and family services—and the resulting necessary, painful reductions in the salaries of our selfless staff, Lilly Endowment provided the resources for us to build our capacity to respond to the unparalleled drug and opioid abuse, a statewide drug epidemic which is bringing more children than ever before into Indiana's child welfare system. The Villages has also been able to fund two full-time social workers, focused exclusively on recruiting, screening, and training desperately-needed foster parents. Further, this endowment has provided crucial training in trauma-informed care for every staff member; assured that The Villages can make long overdue, essential upgrades in our technology; and enabled The Villages to provide vital emergency resources for foster families who are willing to care for the unprecedented number of infant through five-year-olds being removed from their drug-addicted parents. In short, this gift was transformational because Indiana's drug crisis has created a foster care crisis.

The Villages nonprofit world is surrounded with choppy waters, but our mission to protect, serve, and affirm vulnerable children propels every member of The Villages family to navigate those waters with patience, perseverance, and with fervor. One of the many lasting gifts my parents embedded in my heart was the gift of optimism. I have learned that the spirit of optimism helps me overcome the most challenging of circumstances, and hopefully, I will pass on that spirit of hope to not only our board and staff but also to the children and families we're so honored to serve.

There is a wonderful, anonymous quote that embodies the tireless spirit of The Villages family: "Do not let today end before you have done something good for someone who will never be able to repay you!"

That's exactly what our board of directors, staff, volunteers, foster and adoptive families, and million-dollar donors do each and every day. They are full partners with The Villages in creating brighter futures.

Lucky us, to be investing in the best future our state will ever have: our children.

About Sharon Pierce

Pierce

Sharon Pierce has served as The Villages' President and CEO since 1992. The Villages, Indiana's largest statewide nonprofit child and family services agency, serving nearly 3,000 children each day, provides foster care, adoption, and family service programs.

Under the leadership of Sharon Pierce, The Villages is among the two percent of child and family service organizations fully accredited by the national Council of Accreditation. It has no incidence of child abuse nor neglect from 99 percent of "first-time" parents served through the agency's Healthy Families program. It also holds a 90-percent annual retention rate of therapeutic foster families, and 89 percent of children served are in only one foster home.

Before joining the organization, Sharon was the Deputy Director for the Indiana Division of Family and Children, overseeing Indiana's state child welfare system. Her experience also includes positions with the Children's Home & Aid Society of Illinois, Youth Advocate Program, Illinois Collaboration on Youth, and Western Michigan University.

Sharon is a member of numerous boards and service organizations promoting the best interests of children. A sampling includes the National Board of Directors for the Child Welfare League of America, where Sharon acts as a National Child Welfare Trainer, the National Board of Directors of Prevent Child Abuse America, and the Indiana Association of Resources and Child Advocacy Institute for Excellence. Sharon has worked with the Indiana General Assembly on numerous legislative initiatives that impact children and families. She served on the Board for Child Care Coordination, the Commission on Abused and Neglected Children, and chaired the Healthy Families Indiana Think Tank.

Sharon's distinguished career has earned her the Department of

Health and Human Services Bi-Annual Commissioner's Award for the State of Indiana, the IARCA Excellence in Service Award, the Pass The Torch For Women Foundation Non-Profit Award, and the Sagamore of the Wabash Award.

She holds a master's degree in student personnel administration and counseling, and a bachelor's degree in English, all from Ball State University, and is an Elder for Zionsville Presbyterian Church.

Sharon is married to Steve Pierce and is the mother of four grown children and grandmother to seven grandchildren.

CHAPTER SEVENTEEN
Ensuring Institutional Success
By Stephen J. Helmich

Like many others who find themselves raising money for life-changing causes, I never thought I would spend much of my working career raising money for life-changing causes. When we were kids answering the question "what do you want to be when you grow up?" few of us respond by jumping on the couch and shouting "fundraiser!"

It is the life-changing aspect of our organizations that gives each of us the courage, stamina, perseverance, and words to do the work many of us never thought we would do or could do. I had not, at the beginning of my nonprofit career, developed my "personal philosophy of money" and had not given much thought to philanthropy or how our family would share our resources with organizations beyond our church. I certainly held that same fear of "making the 'ask'" shared by so many in our field. Very little in my life, to that point in time, would suggest I was ready to make a real detour in my career and spend much of my time asking people to invest in a cause.

Then I was selected to be president of Cathedral High School in Indianapolis, Indiana. I am still a bit shocked I was given the opportunity to do this work. I was not a graduate of Cathedral. I did not live in Indianapolis. Although Catholic, I had never attended a Catholic high school as none existed in my hometown. I am not convinced I could have created, at the moment I was hired, a compelling list of the ten most important things a president of a Catholic high school must do to ensure institutional success.

It did not take very long to realize that asking for money would easily be at the top of the list for me and most Catholic high school presidents.

Cathedral is the largest and oldest Catholic high school in Indiana. It was founded in 1918 to provide a high school education to young men from diverse ethnic backgrounds in post-World War I Indianapolis. Today, it is a private co-educational Catholic high school of 1,210 young men and women serving the entirety of central Indiana.

The original school building was located in downtown Indianapolis from 1918 until the mid-1970s. The founding teachers and administrators were Holy Cross Brothers, an order of Brothers with roots at the University of Notre Dame. The mission story for Cathedral clearly had its roots with the Brothers and the Congregation of Holy Cross. This religious order was, and is, a gathering of remarkable men absolutely committed to their faith, to young people, and to providing an extraordinary educational experience that will allow young people to be prepared to see the challenges and opportunities that face their society and to take action to effect the changes they are capable of making. "The competence to see and the courage to act" are remarkable words that define a Holy Cross education. This mission is intact at Cathedral 100 years after its founding. This mission resonated for me and certainly has so for many thousands of graduates over the years. Mission, I am convinced, is the primary source of our courage, stamina, perseverance, and words.

But Cathedral, in the late 1960s and early 1970s, was in crisis. Enrollment was declining as families with school-age children in the center city were moving to the suburbs. There were fewer Brothers to staff the Holy Cross high schools in the Midwest and, with Cathedral's declining enrollment, it was announced that Cathedral High School would close.

The last minute efforts of a small group of passionate Cathedral graduates allowed the school to remain open as a private Catholic institution. This truly heroic effort in salvation is an almost mythical story that has been told and retold by members of the Cathedral family. And these efforts to save the school will prove to play a very important role in future years as philanthropy becomes a critical component of initially saving the school, and then securing the investments that will be necessary to allow the school to become one of the very best Catholic high schools in the Midwest, and, the country. These mythical stories will prove to impact future generations of school supporters and encourage these men and women to do whatever is necessary to allow the school to survive, grow, and thrive.

This initial group of Cathedral zealots wrote personal checks and raised money so that an all-girls Catholic academy campus on the northeast side of Indianapolis could be purchased. The school became a coeducational institution. Not all of the boys or girls embraced this change, and the early days of the coeducational school were challenging to say the least.

The importance of stories will become clear in the development of the high-performing school Cathedral has become. Early supporters of the school deposited personal checks in the school's checking account every two weeks so that payroll could be met. The president of the new Cathedral cleaned bathrooms and classrooms on the weekend. Teachers were occasionally told to not cash their checks on Friday, but to wait until Monday when the weekend's bingo profits could be deposited. The early days of the new Cathedral were most challenging and each of these early years brought questions as to whether the school could really survive and prosper.

Folks who raise money for a living, or serve as an enlightened board member, often talk about a "culture of philanthropy." Other than the school-saving efforts of the dedicated alumni, there was no established culture of philanthropy at Cathedral. The Brothers had served as a living endowment, working for room and board. Bingo was the lead fundraising activity. No comprehensive advancement efforts had been undertaken from the founding in 1918 to the saving of the school in the 1970s. No advancement efforts had been needed as the downtown school building was paid for, and the Brothers, with their vow of poverty, kept the overhead of the school very, very low. Tuition, for many years, was "$50, if you could afford it."

Some real fundraising progress had been made in the 1980s. A campaign was held to help retire the mortgage for the new campus. Another campaign was held to raise funds to build a much needed gymnasium.

But the winds of change were in the air. New high schools were opening. Some of these would be faith-based schools. Some of these new schools would eventually be public charter schools which operated very much as a private school would operate and were free.

Public schools were improving their performance and were proving to be viable options for young families challenged by the ever-increasing tuitions at private high schools.

In early 2000, a strategic plan was undertaken by Cathedral's board, staff, and school community. I had arrived in the spring of 1999. The plan was effectively completed, and to no one's surprise, a substantial amount of money was required to fund the plan. A new library and student life center, significant investments in information technology, an upgrade in athletic facilities, increased pay for teaching faculty, and more money for need-based tuition assistance were major pieces of this plan. It was truly felt that Cathedral must make these investments at this moment in time if the school was to move forward and pursue an oft-repeated goal of being "the great American Catholic high school." The price tag for the plan was nearly twenty million dollars, nearly fifteen million dollars more than the school had raised in any of the previous campaigns.

It was very clear we were going to need to accelerate the process of building a culture of philanthropy at the school. We were not going to have the luxury of executing a text book strategy of meeting, nurturing, and stewarding our prospective donors. There were certainly a core of Cathedral loyalists who understood the need and were prepared to be asked. But, the size, scope, and time-critical aspect of this twenty million dollar effort would require many new donors to hear the case for support and respond "yes!" when asked for an investment.

There was clearly a sense of urgency amongst the board members and key staff. The strategic planning process had exposed some weaknesses that had to be addressed. The strategic planning process had made all of us more keenly aware of our competition and the steps our competition was taking in efforts to attract students and families that had historically made Cathedral their school of choice.

We knew there were not enough individuals to make a $250 gift to the school to ensure the $20 million campaign would be successful. We also knew there were hundreds of highly successful alumni spread across the country. Some of these individuals had graduated from the new Cathedral that opened in the 1970s on the northeast side of

Indianapolis. But many of these highly successful alumni had graduated from the downtown school, and had been taught by the Brothers. Many of these highly successful, high net worth, graduates had little to no direct contact with the school or current school leadership.

There was a question, in our early planning stages, as to whether these more mature graduates, many who had spent their entire post-college careers in cities other than Indianapolis, would demonstrate that their loyalty and commitment to the school would cause them to make the six- and seven-figure gifts that would be necessary to ensure success. We did know, through our feasibility study process, that many of these more mature alumni had remained in close contact with their classmates. Many shared, "that their best and closest friends were Cathedral friends. We found a remarkable appreciation of the Holy Cross Brothers. These religious men and educators clearly had life changing impact on many of our mature graduates. And, it was clear that the "competence to see and courage to act" mission of the school had been embraced by these alumni. Many of these individuals had rightfully earned the reputation as a top community leader in the city they had called home during their adult lives.

Our strategy, by necessity of time and this growing sense of urgency, bypassed the fully deployed moves management model. We identified high net worth Cathedral graduates around the country. We did our very best to know as much as we could about each donor prospect. We looked for possible links to the modern Cathedral and did our best to establish family or friend ties with school. We did our research to find their philanthropic interests and their giving history to Cathedral.

We wished we had more time. We wished we could delay for two or three years to have time for meetings, lunches, and dinners with donor prospects. But, we did not feel, at this moment in the school's history, we had the luxury of time, and that the clock was ticking at a rate that suggested we move forward with a campaign.

We did have very effective counsel, and an appreciation this was not the best way to run a campaign. But, we were emboldened by the feedback we were receiving from a number of the graduates we met during some trips around the country. We were moved by the stories they told about their Cathedral experience, their affection for their classmates, and their deep respect and appreciation regarding their teachers, the Bothers of Holy Cross. There were quite a few tears shed by these mature community leaders as they shared their own, very personal stories of the impact of the school on their lives.

So we secured lead gifts from the locals who had remained close to the school and who we knew were committed to this campaign. A stirring moment occurred when the general chairman of the campaign met with Cathedral faculty and staff to announce his family's one million dollar initial investment. A local endowment informed the school shortly after the chairman's announcement that it would invest two million dollars in our campaign.

But we knew the campaign's success still would be determined by the answers from the many very successful alumni whose loyalty to the school would be tested as we met to ask for their support for this mission-critical fundraising effort.

Michael J. Conaton provided a "million-dollar moment" for the school very early in the campaign. His gift was obviously extraordinarily significant because of its size and use, but the timing and the positive impact of his gift on other alumni was impossible to calculate.

Mike graduated from Cathedral in 1952. He played football and was a top student. He chose to continue his football career at Xavier University in Cincinnati, Ohio, and Cincinnati became his home. And, like many others on our prospecting radar, he had only minimal contact with Cathedral after graduation.

Mike had a monumental business career, and an equally impressive career as a community leader in his city. He had served as board chair for every important community organization and cause. He had served as chairman of the board of trustees at Xavier University for nearly twenty years. They simply would not let Mike step down as board chair. He was just that good, and had that kind of very special impact on the university he cared for so deeply.

I contacted Mike and asked if I could meet with him in Cincinnati. Like so many of the very successful men and women I have gotten to know through my work, I found Mike to be not only very successful, but also gracious and very humble. He struck me, immediately, as one of the finest men I was going to have the opportunity to get to know.

I was aware of some of the challenges before me. Mike did not have a deep and intimate relationship with his high school. He was extraordinarily loyal to Xavier University, and this included very significant investments, over time, to Xavier. Buildings on the campus bore his name. He was very philanthropic, and other organizations and causes in Cincinnati had benefited from Mike's philanthropy.

But I could sense that he had strong feelings about Cathedral, his experience there, and the positive impact of a Holy Cross education. Mike, like a number of graduates I met with, shared the sentiment that "I would not be who I am, or where I am today, if not for Cathedral and the Brothers." I was hopeful that Mike would entertain a discussion about the school at that moment in time, the very effective strategic planning that had been accomplished, the urgency that leadership was feeling about investing in the campus and her people, and his interest in participating in the campaign.

Mike was agreeable to engaging in that conversation. And, on my second visit to Cincinnati to meet with Mike, he gave us a million-dollar moment. The Michael J. Conaton Library is an important part of the campus that created the environment that so effectively nurtures learning and growing at the school.

Ours certainly was not a perfect campaign strategy. We did not take the time many experts would suggest is important, and some might say, critical, to meet with and nurture prospective donors. What we did come to understand was there was tremendous appreciation for Cathedral held by virtually every graduate with whom we had a conversation. Story after story was told of lives being forever changed by the Cathedral experience. We increasingly felt that, given the number of successful graduates and the compelling story we had to tell about our Choice of Futures Campaign, we could build a gift pyramid that was legitimate and would ensure a successful campaign. We determined this loyalty and passion for the school might overcome a less-than-remarkable process of nurturing.

We made it true that those same mythical stories told over all the years of the school's history would serve us well. We told about Bishop Chartrand raising one million dollars on a single Sunday in 1917 to build the original school building. We told of times when teachers would wait till Monday to cash their check so that bingo deposits could be cleared, and we reminded donor prospects of times when board members and others deposited personal checks every two weeks so that expenses could be met. Many of the donors remembered these stories and remembered the challenges the school faced when they were enrolled. Many many prospective donors were interested in helping their school not only succeed, but also become "the great American high school."

I suppose people can debate until the cows come home why people give money. I am convinced, beginning with this first campaign I was involved with, that people give money to positively change lives. Certainly people see "changing lives" in different ways. For some, it may be an opportunity to view a piece of art, for others it might be clean water, and, thankfully for some, it was providing an education that would help some of tomorrow's leaders develop "the competence to see and the courage to act."

About Steve Helmich

Steve Helmich, former President of Cathedral High School in Indianapolis, retired as the first President of the Indiana High School Athletic Association Foundation. In his role as chief administrator, Helmich oversaw the day-to-day operations of the Foundation, including the development and fundraising efforts to support its programs and distribution of scholarships and grants.

Steve joined the Association following a sixteen-year career as President of Cathedral High School, where he led one of the largest Catholic, private, independent high schools in the Midwest.

Included in his many responsibilities was serving as chief fundraiser for the institution where his efforts resulted in nearly three million dollars annually for the Cathedral Fund and oversight of four highly-

Helmich

successful capital campaigns during his tenure.

In addition, Steve was influential in the development of Cathedral's Advanced Placement program, which offers 27 courses, the International Baccalaureate Programme, the iPad 1:1 Program, and the Cathedral 360 Personalized Education Experience. He headed up the 2011 initiative to reaffiliate with the Brothers of Holy Cross, the original teaching order from the school's founding in 1918 through to its move to the current campus on 56th Street in 1975.

He is affiliated with three boards of directors: the Center for Leadership Development, OneAmerica Fund, and the Damar Foundation. He previously was affiliated with the Indiana Non Public Education Association.

Prior to Cathedral, Steve served as President of the Community Education Coalition in Columbus, Indiana, and President and CEO of the Columbus Area Chamber of Commerce. He also worked as President and CEO of the Richmond-Wayne County Chamber of Commerce, and Executive Director of the Richmond Family YMCA.

A graduate of Indiana University, Steve earned Big Ten All-Academic honors in football as he obtained a bachelor's degree in Education and a master's degree in Secondary Education. He went on to spend twelve years as a classroom teacher and coach across Indiana, including Noblesville, West Lafayette, Richmond, and Columbus North high schools.

Steve is married to Cynthia. The Helmichs have three daughters: Carrie, Amy, and Nastya.

.

CHAPTER EIGHTEEN
Bill and My Million-Dollar Moment
By Vance Peterson

From Toledo to Tahoe

When I was a professor and director of the John H. Russel Center for the Study of Higher Education at the University of Toledo, I never thought fundraising would have such an impact on my career.

I never gave it a second thought when I majored in English literature at Occidental College, when I received my Master of Science in Administration from George Washington University, and, especially, when I earned my PhD from Stanford in Administration and Policy Analysis.

However, life is full of many unexpected twists and turns, and life introduces you to many interesting people. In this case, his name was Bill. Bill became the focal point of my million-dollar moment.

Along Came Bill

Bill became an important part of my life in the mid-1990s, more than twenty years after I entered the field of higher education, and shortly after I became President of Sierra Nevada College. Those two decades included stops at the University of Southern California (USC), the University of California at Los Angeles (UCLA), and Occidental College after the University of Toledo.

Working directly for the Provost at USC, my prime responsibilities as Director of Academic Relations were communications and rebranding the University as an increasingly formidable private R1 institution. Communications and rebranding were also prime emphases when I moved to UCLA as Director of Campaign Operations. This is where I cut my teeth in the field of resource development. While at UCLA, my career continued on an upward path. I was promoted to Associate Provost, College of Arts and Sciences and Associate Director of

University Relations, focusing, by then, almost entirely on fundraising.

My alma mater, Occidental College, then called in 1990, and I accepted the position of Vice President for Advancement. Serving my undergraduate alma mater was a special opportunity, and we successfully completed a $72 million campaign.

Although I didn't realize it when I first joined USC, each subsequent step contributed immeasurably to my understanding of advancement as an integrated, multidisciplinary team endeavor, and helped prepare me for my first encounter with Bill several years later.

Sierra Nevada College was 28 years old when I became its President. Located at Lake Tahoe, Nevada, it is surrounded by magnificent scenery throughout the year. The college offers a truly unique educational experience for its students. As we used to say, it brings "the inspiration of Lake Tahoe into every classroom through an active model of teaching that provokes transformative learning moments...the kind that lead to self-knowledge, confidence, and success."

Seeking to be true to our mission and wanting to recruit a special type of student, the college undertook a focused strategic planning process. Our strategic plan called for next steps in the buildout of our new campus near the lake, and, in particular, the library envisioned in the campus master plan to be the signature building on our campus. All we needed was a donor to make the library a reality.

I first met Bill at a fundraising dinner, ironically one sponsored by another nonprofit organization in town. We instantly clicked, and I was fascinated, with growing admiration and respect, as the personal story of this sincere and likeable octogenarian began to unfold.

Bill was a pilot in World War II. As a young man, he had flown 34 missions over Europe in a B-17 Bomber. As the conversation progressed, he shared in his modest, matter-of-fact way fascinating and vivid stories about several of those missions. After the war, Bill became a successful developer. "I build things," he told me. He said he felt most alive and fulfilled whenever he was bringing a new building or major new development to life.

As President of a young and growing liberal arts college, which recently had acquired a valuable parcel of land on which to build a new main campus, I thought Bill might have some interest in what we were doing. I invited Bill to come and see our master plan, and give me his thoughts about it. I was hoping to tap into his expertise as a developer, but certainly, also, to introduce him to the college and our dreams for the future.

Fortunately, I had the good counsel and guidance of a planning team that included Jane Rohrer, Vice President of Academic Affairs; Diane Severance, Planning Consultant; and Bruce James, future Chairman of the Sierra Nevada Board of Trustees. This group was my "kitchen cabinet" and sounding board for strategy and cultivation regarding Bill.

Meeting the Needs of Both College and Donor

As it turned out, our strategy and cultivation was extremely important because of something we discovered in the cultivation process. Bill's life was shaped by his service, his business, and his personal tragedy. The death of his fourteen-year-old son, about which he said very little, either when we met or throughout the process, had left an obvious and unhealed wound on his heart. He told me later, in an unguarded moment, that the memory of his son was the primary reason he cared so much about helping youth. He saw the college and the library as his connection with his late son.

Sierra Nevada College was operating at two campuses at the time. In order for Bill to see the whole picture and a potential before and after scenario, Bill and I decided to see both campuses. We began our tour on the old campus which ended at the library: a cramped, A-frame structure bursting at the seams with books and journals, which housed only two student study carrels. I shared with Bill that a new library was the centerpiece of our new campus design, and my highest current priority, following the recent construction of a residence hall and dining hall. With its integral classrooms, room for growth of the collection, a gallery, faculty offices, and ample student-study space, the new library would enable us to move the entirety of our operations to the new campus upon completion.

Bill had rarely, if ever, spent any time in a library, but it wasn't hard for him to see the problem the college was facing. While his first inclination was to help us find a way to add on to the existing structure, Bill was open to learning more about details for the library on the new campus and how it would dramatically transform the college and the student experience.

Following many subsequent conversations and interactions, including at our weekly poker and beer night (Bill became part of our group), this very soft-spoken, low-key gentleman, in a face-to-face meeting, pledged the lead gift to build and partially endow the new library.

I'll never forget my reaction. My first thoughts were admiration and respect for Bill. Then, there was elation for the future of Sierra Nevada College. And, for one fleeting moment, I was pleased to have accomplished something special in my professional capacity. As for Bill, it was a way to fuse the core elements of his being. This million dollar moment honored the memory of Bill's son.

I quickly drew up a document which outlined the details of Bill's gift for signature by all involved parties. It was my intention for Bill to be present at the next board of trustees meeting to make his philanthropy public, however, Bill had a conflict. In typical Bill manner, he let me know it was not necessary for his presence at the announcement to the board. It didn't need to be touted.

This dream come true for our students and faculty, as well as Sierra Nevada College as a whole, impacted the entire organization, including our trustees and our donors. For our trustees, it caused them to consider what else they might personally do to advance the college. And, for our donors and alumni beyond the board, it created a great deal of positive buzz and excitement.

In 1996, I was invited to become the president for the Council for the Advancement and Support of Education (CASE), headquartered in Washington, D.C. After I left the college, Bill's story had a completely unanticipated ending.

Lessons Learned

My experience with Bill, both professionally and personally, was an amazing learning opportunity. Here are five items I believe are worth sharing:

Solicitation, The Process — Hearing Bill talk about his World War II experiences, especially the missions he flew over Germany, gave me great insight into a prospective donor who would go on to become a close friend. The friendship was based on Bill, the man: his toughness, his resilience, and his intelligence. Knowing the person's story (in this case what motivated Bill), and understanding who and what impacted his life, was an impetus to discussing our organization's philanthropic needs. Throughout my career in fundraising, and especially since my encounter with Bill, I have felt that opportunities arise most often when one seeks to understand the human being and does more listening than talking.

Solicitation, The Team — Success in an organization is most often the result of we rather than me. As president, I was surrounded by an extraordinary team that crafted a unified direction, always remaining on the same page.

Solicitation, The Ask — There are many people who speak well, but there are far fewer who understand how to ask for the gift. The right words are not spoken. Or worse, the ask is never made or made poorly. I found out a great deal about myself in working with Bill. With the help of my team, I did have the ability to ask for, and close on, a multi-million dollar gift. That is when I knew I had grown as a professional in the field of resource development.

The Result, The Expected — A major gift of this nature lifted the spirits of our faculty, staff, trustees, and contributors. But, what about Bill? It was his way of connecting with a son who had passed away. His philanthropy had not only elevated the confidence of an entire educational community, it also made Bill's heart swell with pride.

The Result, The Unexpected — After I left Sierra Nevada College to become the President of CASE, Bill unfortunately cancelled his pledge after making several initial payments. The reasons for the withdrawal are not important; relationships and understandings change. Sierra Nevada College did receive more than $1.5 million from Bill, and an area of the library was named in his honor. Sadly, not every million-dollar moment has a happy ending. But, that is perhaps best left for another book.

About Vance T. Peterson, PhD

Peterson

Vance T. Peterson is the founding principal of Vance Peterson & Associates, LLC, and a senior consultant for AGB Search where he specializes in advancement leadership searches.

He is Past President of the Council for Advancement and Support of Education and Past President of Sierra Nevada College.

Other professional assignments have included: Vice President for Institutional Advancement at Occidental College; Associate Director of University Development at UCLA; Executive Director of University Relations at the University of Southern California; Adjunct Professor of Higher Education at the University of Pennsylvania; and, Professor of Higher Education and Director of the Center for the Study of Higher Education at the University of Toledo.

His earned degrees include a Bachelor of Arts in English Literature from Occidental College, a Master of Science in Administration from the George Washington University, and a PhD in Administration and Policy Analysis in Higher Education from Stanford University.

Vance is the author of several monographs, book chapters, and articles on advancement and other higher education subjects that have appeared in CASE Currents, Trusteeship Magazine, AGB Reports, *and elsewhere.*

While college and university administration presented many hurdles over a long campus career, Vance did the real thing in college as a 400 meter hurdler where he was world ranked and achieved All-American recognition.

Vance is the father of three daughters and with his wife, Bonnie, recently returned to their original roots in southern California.

CHAPTER NINETEEN
The Unfinished Story
By Byron Tweeten, with Rick Markoff

I was saddened to learn that Byron Tweeten passed away in New York City on Friday, September 1, 2017.

The Chairman and CEO of Growth Design Corporation, Milwaukee, Byron was a special gentleman and a visionary leader. I knew him for 33 years. Along with my father, Byron taught me how to ask for the gift and close major deals with confidence, professionalism, and trust.

His knowledge base was remarkable. Byron was the Founder and Chief Executive Officer of multiple ministries and corporations from Lutheran roots on an Iowa farm to global consulting with ministries of all sizes and missions. He was recently recruited by Emmanuel Church leaders in Naples, Florida, to design, develop, capitalize, and manage a major vision for growing a family of not-for-profits to build integrated communities of faith with combined support services focusing especially on the Latino immigrant cultures from South Florida into Central and South America.

Three of Byron's most significant client accomplishments include a Lilly Endowment-funded redesign and restructuring of eight Christian denomination seminaries into a single coordinated and managed system, the design, planning and organization of a consulting group that ultimately formed 250 fund-development departments for the largest nonprofit nursing home system in America, and the facilitation of a new vision and business model for a Fortune-500-listed fraternal benefit organization providing financial services to its members.

In March 2002, Jossey-Bass Publishers released his book, *Transformational Boards*. He was the recipient of an Honorary Doctor of Law degree from Concordia University in Seward, Nebraska.

Our First Meeting

Two key members of the St. Vincent Medical Center Foundation Board of Trustees, Jerry Bohland and Virgil Gladieux, had previously worked with Byron and Growth Design Corporation on a capital campaign for Siena Heights University in Adrian, Michigan. When another resource development consulting firm conducted an analysis of the giving landscape for St. Vincent Medical Center Foundation in 1984, it concluded the maximum amount that could be raised from such an endeavor was $4.5 million over three years. The results of that study were not satisfactory to all concerned; therefore, Virgil and Jerry suggested I contact Byron.

He was a breath of fresh air. Byron, along with Managing Consultant Frank Habib, came to Toledo in late 1984 to meet with St. Vincent officials. Together, Byron and Frank were everything professed on Growth Design Corporation's website. They focused on relationship building and had a team philosophy and approach to service. They were known for their trust and integrity, listening and communication skills, experience with working with best-in-class not-for-profit organizations, providing solutions and strategies that meet the need, and demonstrating measurable and effective results

The Board, Medical Center officers, and St. Vincent Medical Center Foundation staff developed a strong relationship with Byron, Frank, and the Growth Design team. We spent nearly two years identifying, cultivating, and educating our physicians, employees, donors, and donor prospects. It was determined that our campaign would seek $10 million in cash and deferred gifts over a three year period. That mark was exceeded in the first twelve months.

In large measure, St. Vincent Medical Center Foundation owed much of its campaign success to Byron. The son of a farmer from rural Iowa, Byron was exactly what his company said he was: a recognized authority and strategist around institutional change and transformation. His creative and innovative client solutions, coupled with his personal network of relationships with key leaders in the not-for-profit arena, have set a standard and new model for high-quality services.

Byron And Million Dollar Moments

On May 10, 2017, Byron wrote about a very meaningful million-dollar moment:

First, having had a long and diverse career in Resource Development, I believe all moments are precious and rewarding when someone gives any amount of resource for mission. To be a legitimate facilitator, one must both understand and be the giver.

In the early years on the farm, my mother would say, "here's a dime, go put it in the offering basket!" I enjoyed being a part of a larger giving community.

I also have been a part of eight-and nine-figure requests and financial commitments, complex with multiple benefits, and in the end, transformational and heartwarming at the same time.

The Moment

A small, midwestern Presbyterian University wanted to reestablish its Christian roots and rebuild to a leading private educational institution. The new president, visionary and fearless, suggested to me that we needed several million dollars to launch the largest capital campaign by far in the University's history. He said, "Let's meet a younger board member and ask him for $1 million. Byron, can you mentor me and ask him? I have never asked for a gift of this size and nature before."

I agreed, and after a cocktail at the country club lounge and a chat, the president briefly stated that he wanted to visit about initial capital funding and suggested I lead the conversation. I said that I was there to ask for a lead financial commitment. I stated, "in consideration of fellow board members and alumni, I am asking you to consider a gift in the range of $1 million."

He smiled and said, "Byron and Jim, I will give you $1 million, but what I really want to do is over a period of time, give $20 million. My mentor in the company I now control gave his alma mater $20 million and I want to give my alma mater the same or more."

In the years that followed, he quietly gave much more than $20 million in leadership, talent and gifts for a variety of university initiatives for transforming the campus, new buildings, athletics, fine arts, and curriculum redesign. He was and is a person with a grateful heart, a true visionary and a man of goodwill.

The president became a great resource development leader. I was humbly used as the facilitator in an intimate conversation that created the opportunity for the donor to be transformational.

The Rest of the Story

Byron passed away before he could write the entire story.

His amazing mind not only helped build organizations and strengthen nonprofit missions and visions but also it never ceased to come up with out-of-the-box solutions for the next big thing. One of those big things was the development of waste-to-energy projects.

Byron led the start-up of the Growth Design Energy Division which focused on the integration of multiple waste to renewable energy technologies with energy-intensive businesses to stimulate economic growth. His projects created multiple salable products such as pipeline quality biogas and ammonium sulfate fertilizer; therefore, there was no reliance on government incentives to be profitable. Growth Design Corporation's projects matched technology with available feedstock.

What else could be expected from a man who had a degree in Music Education from Wartburg College, who studied service to the church at Concordia University, who learned about youth ministry at Union Theological Seminary, and who cultivated his interest in educational administration at the University of Wisconsin-Milwaukee?

On his Facebook page, Byron's daughter, Alison, posted the following thought about her father: "So I'm not sure how to say this, and I'm not sure what to say, but my amazing father Byron Tweeten, passed away suddenly September 1st (2017). I miss him so much, and I love him so much. He was such a great dad, and showed me so much of the world. I was so lucky!"

Byron's father, Lehman B. Tweeten, passed away at age 96 in Byron's hometown of Forest City, Iowa, just four years before his son. Byron left this world in his early 70s. Can you imagine what Byron could have accomplished if he lived to be 96?

About Byron Tweeten

Tweeten

Byron L. Tweeten passed away suddenly on September 1, 2017. He was best known as the Founder, Chairman, CEO, and President of Growth Design Corporation, Milwaukee, Wisconsin, which he created in 1981. He served as an advisor to Rick Markoff from 1984 until 2017.

Byron had an impact on many organizations around the world. His knowledge and expertise were well-known. His roles including founder, executive director, manager, CEO, and consultant.

He developed and managed schools, institutes, community-based learning, colleges and universities, including the Next Door Foundation, Finlandia University, John Thomas Dye School, St. Johns Military Academy, Concordia University System, Discovery Institute, Church of Joy and Joy Foundation, and numerous private schools.

His strengths and skills included strategic planning and financial modeling, structuring and team building, funding, communication tools, program design and development, mergers and acquisitions, facilitation of large and small groups, continuous listening and learning, and enterprise development. He handled a range of interesting projects such as The Indiana Pacers Foundation; the largest Goodwills in America; Hazelden Planning, Good Samaritan Long-Term Care Research and Capitalization for 270 Sites; Ecumenical Church Loan Fund Global Micro-Credit; and a Lilly Endowment funded redesign and restructuring of eight Christian denomination seminaries into a single coordinated and managed system.

As a recognized leader in numerous fields, Byron worked with a variety of amazing people whose last names include Annenberg, Simon, and Templeton. He authored Transformational Boards—Engaging Boards and Embracing Change, *published by Jossey-Bass. Byron received an Honorary Doctorate of Law from Concordia University, Seward, Nebraska.*

His educational history included a Bachelor of Arts and Bachelor of Music Education (cum laude) from Wartburg College, and Masters in Educational Leadership, Adult Learning, and Rehabilitation Counseling from the University of Wisconsin, Milwaukee.

Byron will be best remembered as the master of organizational reinvention and process redesign, and for his major philanthropy strategies and initiatives.

Concluding Thoughts, The Magic of a Million-Dollar Gift

Million-Dollar Moments has examined many aspects of million-dollar giving to both the well-known and not so well-known nonprofit organizations across our country and the remarkable stories of eighteen resource development professionals and nonprofit CEOs who described either their first million-dollar moments or their very impactful million-dollar moments. These contributors went into detail concerning their careers, their organizations, the needs of their organizations, their resource development teams and the processes they created, the inner feelings of their donors, their own inner feelings, and the lessons learned from their experiences.

Each item discussed, mission outlined, purpose for giving, and emotion felt is unique to the situation and impactful to the heart. There is much to be learned from each contributor and his or her story. Weaving all of these items together is not easy, but it was a joy to make the attempt.

I have asked a distinguished group of colleagues to put into words the meaning of the magic of a million-dollar gift from their vantage points. Their thoughts are spot-on.

Jerold Panas in his book, *Mega Gifts*, wrote, "...the greatest game possible, the most exhilarating and consequential experience, is the adventure of confronting a potential donor with the opportunity of sharing a great dream." As you have read in the previous pages, for large and for small, dreams, do, indeed, come true.

What do other people who are nonprofit leaders and executives in the resource development industry have to say about the magic of a million-dollar gift?

Gifts of a million dollars or more change small colleges and universities in immeasurable ways. They can initiate permanent change, such as student scholarships forever, new centers for discovery, the recruitment and retention of the very best faculty, long-term facilities updates, science equipment renewal, and so much more.

Those gifts also are the core of raising new funds. A million-dollar gift is always powerful, but at small colleges and universities, they literally change the environment.

Dr. Beverley Pitts
President Emeritus, University of Indianapolis

It was impossible not to cry. On the telephone, the young woman, a senior here at the University of Toledo, was at a crossroads in her life. She was only two semesters away from fulfilling her dream of becoming the first in her family to graduate from college, a major step in the rise from poverty. However, there was a problem, a big problem. Despite holding down a job and going to school full-time, she could no longer afford the cost of college, living expenses, transportation, and food. It was an either-or moment. She chose to pursue her goal, making the decision to live out of her car and finish her degree, in hopes that one more year of sacrifice would change the trajectory of her life's path.

When I called this total stranger to let her know that she had received a major scholarship, she immediately began to open up about the trials and tribulations in her life and how this gift was by far the greatest she had ever received. She was crying. She wasn't the only one.

People ask what it is like to close gifts of six- and seven-figures. It is exhilarating, but not for the reason most imagine. Simply, it is because payments from endowed funds established by generous donors are often the only thing a student and our society have to separate our future from their past.

Dan Saevig
Associate Vice President/Alumni and Annual Engagement
Executive Director, the University of Toledo Alumni Association

I had the pleasure of working with "Judy" on a multi-million dollar gift to create a new collegiate exercise facility. While she had been giving for years, no one had ever spent the time to listen to what was most important to her and where she wanted to make a difference. This gift was the first time she had ever directed her resources to a non-academic endeavor because she felt so strongly about exercise, the body, the mind, and health for young people. At the dedication, she cried tears of joy, and the students cried with her and watched in amazement as this wonderful woman broke down over the impact of her gift and the number of students she would positively affect for decades to come.

Sheri Gladden
Amherst College
Washington University, St. Louis
Smith College
Mount Holyoke College
Methodist Health Foundation
Indiana University-Purdue University Indianapolis

When I think of the magic of a million, I picture a beautiful tapestry. The magic begins with the heart. It is the moment when the donor gives their heartfelt passion and generosity to help lift up a charity's needs and bring their own philanthropic vision to fruition. It is like weaving beautiful patterns into a tapestry where the donor's passion and generosity are the threads. The charity provides the weaving and the tapestry is the need. This beautiful tapestry is a cascading plan that makes hearts swell while making an impactful, meaningful difference in the lives of so many in need. It creates a legacy by becoming a part of the fabric of the community and wrapping its magic around the hearts of so many to provide life for generations to come.

Proverbs 3:6 says, "Seek His will in all you do, and He will show you which path to take."

Trish Oman Clark
Executive Director,
The Leukemia & Lymphoma Society, Indiana Chapter

The environment of the million-dollar investment may occur through a cultivated relationship, or a single situational driven event. In most cases, the use of this gift is donor determined and driven; however, institutional input will occur. The recognition of the gift involves the donor and the institution. Finally, the most critical component is the fulfilment of the investment's purpose which builds the relationship between the donor and the institution.

Jon Labahn
Principal, Strategic Resource Management, Ltd., Naples, Florida

I am always amazed by the unexpected million-dollar gift. Picture a married couple that has lived in the same home for decades where they raised their family and are deeply involved in their community. They tend to be quiet, encouraging, and possess family values that have helped lead to their success. They get excited by the energy a charity's mission creates and are just waiting to be asked. They know they do not fit the typical millionaire mold, but they are proud of the difference they know their gift will make. They are looking for a way to pass along resources that match their values. The fun part of my job is to get to know them well enough to be allowed the honor of inviting them to share their resources and help them create a legacy for the future. Every time it happens I feel like I have helped them find great satisfaction and peace. I've got the best job.

Ken File
President, Damar Foundation, Indianapolis, Indiana

We met in the office of an icon in our community. I was humbled that he could find time to meet us given his responsibilities and the general demands on his time. Here was a man who had already been so generous to our organization over the course of a relationship that spanned decades. I went over my vision for the organization, what we hoped to accomplish for our community, and discussed how he might help. Our discussion concluded with a request that he consider a transformational eight-figure gift, a gift that would be the first of its kind to our organization. After consideration, he gladly committed to the gift saying, "I've always been a great fan of United Way, but if you hadn't asked for this transformational gift, I would have continued with a smaller gift." Yet more proof that you don't get what you don't ask for!

Ann Murtlow
President and CEO, United Way of Central Indiana

The impact of seven- and eight-figure gifts can be huge, of course. They propel the university toward the achievement of objectives that would be completely out of reach without them. But, there is a need to balance the publicity we create to recognize them and the effect they have on donors. To those who can give seven- and eight-figure gifts, they validate need and the credibility of the institution in securing them. But, to those who cannot give at that level, they can cause a question all development officers must confront. "With such big gifts, my gift won't make any difference, so why should I bother? I can give to another cause that really needs me." We must do all we can to avoid that reaction, even if it relatively isolated. One way to feature such gifts is to aggregate the total dollars received from all gifts of $1,000, or less, in a year. Another is to point out that a gift of $1,000 is the equivalent of the payout of a $20,000 endowment for a year. Still another is to recognize the gifts of a particular constituency over time.

Curt Simic
President Emeritus, Indiana University Foundation

One day, a man sitting at lunch with me removed a wallet-size checkbook from his pocket and began filling out a check. Then, apologizing for not having an envelope, he handed me a check for a million dollars. It was only then that he gave me a career-shifting gift. He said, "You probably thought that we weren't very interested in your project. We are, though, and I want to thank you for asking us."

Sam J. Kennedy CFRE
President and Principal, Strategic Partners, Inc.

Through the last three years of running a small start-up nonprofit, I have been working diligently to build organizational structure to fulfil our foundation's mission. My work and my team's work is considered servant leadership, but my goal is to take our services nationally. If we were to receive a blessing of a million-dollar gift, we would be able to impact so many student lives in urban communities around the nation.

Blake Nathan
CEO and Founder, Educate ME Foundation, INC

Million-dollar gifts have the power to influence and shape trends in philanthropy. Within higher education, health, arts, basic needs, and more recently in the environment and international subsectors, million-dollar gifts are transforming approaches to providing public goods, solving intractable problems, and fueling innovation. Large gifts by individuals, foundations, and corporations have attracted significant media and public attention. Recent policy debates on growing wealth and income inequality in the US have led to a great deal of interest in the large-scale philanthropy. In the US, million dollar gifts account for a significant share of US charitable dollars. The 2016 *Million Dollar Donors Report* found that 1,823 million-dollar gifts were given within the US in 2015, with the total value of the donations at $19.3 billion.[9] The total value of these gifts constitute nearly five percent of the $390.05 billion total estimated for charitable giving during 2016.[10] But large-scale philanthropy is also growing in other parts of the globe, particularly in Asia and Latin America where wealth is growing.

Philanthropy, particularly million-dollar gifts, can play a key role in fueling scientific advances, or serving as a catalyst for research in new areas in health, education, environment, and other key sectors. Philanthropic support also fuels innovation in how services are delivered and can raise awareness around local and global health issues such as HIV/AIDS and malaria.

Dr. Una Osili

Professor of Economics and Associate Dean for Research and International Programs, Lilly Family School of Philanthropy

BONUS CHAPTER
Magical Names in Philanthropic History

Million-dollar gifts are in the grasp of numerous nonprofit organizations today. Gifts that are made by individuals from all walks of life, not just those who have made extraordinary fortunes. That is a focus of our eighteen stories, and the stories of the women and men who helped make these million-dollar moments become a reality.

My fascination with the magic of million-dollar gifts began in the mid-1980s and has grown stronger with every passing annual fund drive, major special event, capital campaign, and planned gift. It flourishes when I discover the stories behind the stories while engaging in conversation with wonderful and dedicated professionals who make nonprofit organization leadership and resource development for those nonprofits their life's vocation.

This fascination is shared by numerous resource development professionals, nonprofit executives, educators, board members, volunteers, and many Americans from every walk of life. One of the best explanations I encountered about our fascination with the million-dollar gift came from Jacquie Ackerman, Assistant Director for Research and Partnerships, Women's Philanthropy Institute, Lilly Family School of Philanthropy. She told me: "A million-dollar gift is a mental threshold. It is an astronomical number to the average American. Most donors appear on The Million-Dollar List once… normally a legacy gift 'to the world.'"

David C. Hammack, Haydn Professor of History, Case Western Reserve University, a past president of the Association for Research on Nonprofit Organizations and Voluntary Action, and 2012 recipient of the Association's award for distinguished achievement, provided me with a historical insight of the word millionaire. He said one might consider that "millionaire" became a notable term only towards the end of the nineteenth century. The earliest use of the term, according to the Oxford English Dictionary, occurred in 1795.

Further, Dr. Hammack said some of America's richest people did make large gifts that likely exceeded $1 million in today's dollars. There are various studies of the richest Americans; Sigmund Diamond's "Reputation of the American Businessmen" might be useful because it is based on a careful study of every obituary of the wealthiest man to die in each 20-year period from about 1800 to 1950. Before the Civil War some very large gifts went to the Astor Library in New York, the Philadelphia orphanage known as Girard College, or Boston's Lowell Institute.

Higher Education in Transition, by John S. Brubacher and Willis Rudy, documents revenues and resources in early America. Between the Revolutionary and Civil Wars, the record discloses only about a dozen large gifts for the use of higher learning, and these ranged from $20,000 to $175,000. When Princeton made a drive in 1830 for $100,000, an ambitious undertaking in those days, the largest single gift was $5,000. Ezra Cornell started the college that bears his name with $500,000, thus in a single gift matching the total endowment of all colleges at the start of the century. In 1873, Cornelius Vanderbilt gave $1 million for the institution eventually named after him. Also in 1873, Johns Hopkins bequeathed $7 million to start Johns Hopkins University in Baltimore. Here, in a single gift, was an endowment which matched the endowment it had taken Harvard almost 250 years to accumulate.

Greater munificence was yet to come. Stanford University commenced with a memorial gift from Leland Stanford in 1885 and the University of Chicago ultimately became the beneficiary of $600,000 from John D. Rockerfeller in 1890.

In the twentieth century, "not millions, but now hundreds of millions of dollars were poured into philanthropic foundations by men like Carnegie, Rockefeller, and Ford, to mention but three of the notable givers."[11]

With this background, I embarked on a search of million-dollar gift giving in America. It would be easy to discover enough information to write an encyclopedia on the subject. That was not my intention. Instead, I found myself having favorite "rainmakers" in the history of million-dollar gifts in our country, 36 in all. I introduce them to you in chronological order, from the first actual million dollar gift I researched to multi-million dollar acts of philanthropy by names found in Forbes and Fortune Magazines today.

The 1800s

1835, James Smithson—I could not find a true million dollar moment in my research until I stumbled upon James Smithson, and, the moment was almost unexplainable. It was not until 1835, six years after his death, that the United States government was informed about the bequest of James Smithson. Martin Morse Wooster described Smithson's trailblazing gift. The Englishman set forth in his will that he "bequeath the whole of my property… to the United States of America, to found at Washington, under the name of the Smithsonian Institution, an establishment for the increase and diffusion of knowledge among men." His generosity amounted to $508,318.46. Another $54,165.38 would arrive some years later. His philanthropy created the Smithsonian Museums in Washington, D.C. Adjusted for inflation, the initial portion of Smithson's gift was in excess of $12.9 million in today's dollars.

1848, John Jacob-Astor—"Before financier John Jacob Astor died in 1848, he worked with the book collector and librarian Joseph Green Cogswell to lay the groundwork, with a gift of $400,000, for a great public library," the Astor Library. Today, it is known as the New York Public Library. "Within two months of Astor's death, the trustees— including Cogswell, Washington Irving, writer Fitz-Greene Halleck, and Samuel Ruggles, the developer of Gramercy Park—met to develop specific plans." The Astor Library opened its doors in 1849. The $400,000 gift from John Jacob-Astor in 1848 was worth $11.6 million in 2015.

1848, Stephen Girard—In an op-ed in the Jan. 2, 1997 edition of *The Wall Street Journal*, Stephen Girard was described as "the Father of Philanthropy." The piece went onto say, "Along with John Jacob-Astor, Girard personally financed the War of 1812 for the U.S. Government."[12] The history of Girard College, a boarding school for children from poor families headed by single parents or guardians, reflects the history of Philadelphia and the nation. Opened in 1848, Girard College was established under a bequest from Girard, who died seventeen years earlier. He specified in his will that "a college for poor white male orphans" would be the result of his bequest which amounted to $7 million.[13] Challenges to the bequest by family members were contested in court for most of those seventeen years. By the mid-twentieth century the expansion of Philadelphia's black population and the quest for civil rights led to the desegregation of Girard College. In 1968, mass protests and litigation succeeded in opening the doors to African-American children.

1853, Judah Touro—In 1853, the final year of his life, Judah Touro wrote his last will and testament, setting a standard for American philanthropy. After modest bequests to various family members, Touro donated half of his fortune to strengthen Jewish life in America. He left $100,000 to the two congregations and various Jewish benevolent associations in New Orleans. Another $150,000 was divided among Jewish congregations and charitable institutions in eighteen other cities throughout the United States, providing support for virtually every traditional synagogue then existing in America. He directed that $50,000 be used to relieve poverty and provide freedom of worship for Jews in Palestine. The remaining half of his bequests went to non-Jewish causes such as the Massachusetts General Hospital, which his brother, Abraham, helped found.[14] In today's dollars, a $50,000 donation in 1853 is worth $1.5 million.

1861, Matthew Vassar—Education philanthropy over the first century of American history was focused predominantly on young men until Matthew Vassar came along. He was determined to use the fortune he accumulated from a self-made career in business to establish "a college for young women which shall be to them what Yale and Harvard are to young men." Milo Jewett, a clergyman who had founded the Judson Female Institute in Alabama in 1839, encouraged Vassar on this endeavor, appealing "to his desire to serve mankind, his local pride, his Christian faith," according to historian Merle Curti.[15] In 1861, Vassar presented to the future Board of Trustees a tin box containing stock and bond certificates valued at $408,000, plus a deed to 200 acres near Poughkeepsie, New York. This gift, along with an additional $400,000 offered before his death, plus continued support from the Vassar family, was the power behind one of the world's first women's colleges offering a broad liberal education. Matthew Vassar's donation also marked a new era in college philanthropy, shifting from subscriptions by many donors toward major gifts from individuals. In today's dollars, $408,000 in 1861 is equal to nearly $10.4 million.

1865, Ezra Cornell—The founding of Cornell University brought together all of the themes that were important in Ezra Cornell's life: his deep and abiding concern for education, his interest in agriculture, his philanthropic impulse, and his political sense.[16] After much political maneuvering, a bill was passed in the New York Assembly, April 21, 1865, in the New York Senate one day later, and signed by Governor Reuben E. Fenton on April 27, which gave birth to Ezra Cornell's dream of a great public university. The first meeting of the Board of Trustees was held on April 28. "Cornell endowed the university through an outright gift of $500,000, to which would be added the sum realized by Cornell's purchase of the Morrill land scrip from the state."[17] Ezra Cornell's vision enabled the University to enroll African-Americans and students from countries outside the United States. "…I trust we have laid the foundation of an University—an institution where any person can find instruction in any study."[18] In today's dollars, $500,000 in 1865 is equal to $7.2 million.

1867, George Peabody—The Peabody Education Fund, established with a $2 million gift from philanthropist George Peabody, was created for the purpose of encouraging education in the post-Civil War American South. "George Peabody is said to have influenced his friends, Johns Hopkins and Enoch Pratt, to establish the famed institutions still in existence that bear their respective names. Other American philanthropists through time, including Rockefeller, Carnegie, and Gates, have also cited Peabody and his model for charitable giving as inspiration for their own giving." During the Fund's existence, its trustees distributed more than $3.5 million in southern states. Liquidated in the 1890s, the majority of the Fund was used to establish what is now Vanderbilt University's George Peabody College for Teachers.[19]

1873, Commodore Cornelius Vanderbilt—The $1 million Commodore Cornelius Vanderbilt gave to endow and build Vanderbilt University was his first and only major philanthropy.[20] The vast majority of the Vanderbilt estate, which totaled $100 million, was bequeathed to his son, William. Commodore Vanderbilt's gift might have never happened if Methodist Bishop Holland N. McTyeire of Nashville, a cousin of the Commodore's young second wife, had not gone to New York for medical treatment early in 1873 and spent time recovering in the Vanderbilt mansion. While there, Bishop McTyeire won the Commodore's admiration and support for building a university in the South that would "contribute to strengthening the ties which should exist between all sections of our common country."[21]

1876, Johns Hopkins—Johns Hopkins University was named for the 19th-century Maryland philanthropist, an entrepreneur and abolitionist with Quaker roots who believed in improving public health and education in Baltimore, and beyond. One of eleven children, Johns Hopkins made his fortune in the wholesale business, and by investing in emerging industries such as the Baltimore and Ohio Railroad. In his will, he set aside $7 million to establish a hospital and affiliated training colleges, an orphanage, and a university. Half of the $7 million created Johns Hopkins University, which opened its doors in 1876. Here in a single gift was an endowment which matched the endowment it had taken Harvard almost 250 years to accumulate.

1884-1891, Leland and Jane Lathrop Stanford—The loss of a child caused a great American educational institution to be born. Railroad magnate and former California Governor Leland Stanford and his wife, Jane Lathrop Stanford, lost their only child, Leland, Jr., to typhoid in 1884. The Stanfords decided to build a university in memory of their son. They deeded an 8,180-acre Palo Alto stock farm to Stanford University. A portion of land subsequently became the campus of the new school. The Stanfords made their plans just as the modern research university was taking form. Leland Stanford Junior University (still its legal name) opened October 1, 1891. Leland

Stanford continued his philanthropy with a historic memorial gift of $20 million. In 1889, Andrew Carnegie wrote, "Perhaps the greatest sum ever given by an individual for any purpose is the gift of Senator Stanford."[22]

1889-1914, John D. Rockefeller, Sr.—John D. Rockefeller, Sr. was the founder of Standard Oil. He made his first gift of $600,000 to the University of Chicago in 1889. "The good lord gave me money. How could I withhold it from Chicago?" he remarked. In all, Rockefeller contributed $35 million to the university.[23] According to the *Chicago Tribune*, the Baptist oil magnate provided the initial funding for the nonsectarian, coeducational institution modeled on the graduate research universities of Germany. Rockefeller and William Rainey Harper, the first president of the university, hoped the school would be a force for Christian moralism in the Midwest at the same time that it developed and promoted modern scientific research. With the support of Rockefeller, the University of Chicago opened in 1892. In 1913, John D. Rockefeller established the Rockefeller Foundation with a gift of $35 million, followed a year later by a gift of $65 million.[24]

1890, Mary Elizabeth Garrett—"To this lady, more than any other single person, save only Johns Hopkins himself, does the School of Medicine owe its being." These are the words of Alan Chesney in his history of the Johns Hopkins School of Medicine.[25] Dedicated to promoting financial and political independence for women, heiress and Bryn Mawr College founder Mary Elizabeth Garrett offered Johns Hopkins University a gift of $307,000 to establish a medical school, with several stipulations, including one that required the program accept women. Her strategy succeeded. Mary Elizabeth Garrett also enlisted the services of other leadings women of philanthropy, including Mrs. J. Pierpont Morgan, Mrs. Leland Stanford, and First Lady Mrs. Benjamin Harrison, to help her raise funds for the School of Medicine.[26] Garrett's 1890 donation of $307,000 would be valued at more than $7.9 million in today's dollars.

1897, Levi Strauss—One of the most iconic names in the world of retail is Levi Strauss. In 1897, he funded 28 scholarships at the University of California, Berkeley, half of which were awarded to women. He was also one of San Francisco's greatest philanthropists. Levi was a contributor to the Pacific Hebrew Orphan Asylum and Home, the Eureka Benevolent Society and the Hebrew Board of Relief. His philanthropy totaled in the millions of dollars. Upon his death in 1902, the San Francisco Board of Trade created a special resolution, which, in part, reads, "the great causes of education and charity have likewise suffered a signal loss in the death of Mr. Strauss, whose splendid endowments to the University of California will be an enduring testimonial to his worth as a liberal, open-minded citizen and whose numberless, unostentatious acts of charity in which neither race nor creed were recognized, exemplified his broad and generous love for and sympathy with humanity."

The 1900s

1901-1919, John Andrew Carnegie—Andrew Carnegie was a self-made giant in the steel industry. Born in Scotland, he built then sold Carnegie Steel Corporation to United States Steel Corporation in 1901. By the time he died in 1919, he is believed to have given away over $350 million.[27] Andrew Carnegie had made some charitable donations before 1901, but after that time, giving his money away became what seemed to be his full-time occupation. In 1902 he founded the Carnegie Institution (now Carnegie-Mellon University) to fund scientific research and established a pension fund for teachers with a $10 million donation. Earlier, he contributed $5 million to the New York Public Library, and in 1905, Carnegie created The Carnegie Foundation for the Advancement of Teaching. "It is said that more than 2,800 libraries were opened with his support."[28]

1907, Margaret Olivia Sage—Upon the death of her husband, Wall Street millionaire Russell Sage (1816-1906), Margaret Olivia Sage committed his fortune to philanthropy. In 1907 she endowed the Russell Sage Foundation, dedicated to applying the social sciences to develop effective, systemic solutions to social problems (the improvement of social and living conditions in the United States). It was America's first private family foundation. Margaret Sage was also a strong proponent of women in higher education. Prime beneficiaries of her giving in this sector were Syracuse, Cornell, Princeton, and a grant which made possible the opening of Russell Sage College.

1912-1920, George Eastman—George Eastman's first camera was called the Kodak, the impetus for the manufacturing giant he founded in 1888, the Eastman Kodak Company of Rochester, New York. In an effort to support his employees, he developed what is known as the stock option.[29] He had a great admiration for the Massachusetts Institute of Technology (MIT), particularly because he gained many talented assistants from the ranks of their graduates. Using the pseudonym of Mr. Smith, Eastman anonymously donated more than $22 million to MIT over an eight year period.[30] Additional seven figure contributions went to the University of Rochester, Rochester Institute of Technology, Hampton University, and Tuskegee Institute. Without fanfare, Eastman also set up free dental clinics for children in Rochester and cities in Europe where Eastman Kodak factories operated.[31]

1912-1932, Julius Rosenwald—Capitalizing on his understanding of how to utilize the mail order business, Julius Rosenwald was able to go from suit maker to the president of the Sears Roebuck & Company.[32] "In 1912, Rosenwald made a dramatic entry into large-scale philanthropy. He announced he would be celebrating his 50th birthday by giving away close to $700,000 (about $16 million in current dollars) and encouraged other wealthy individuals to support good causes of their own. 'Give While You Live,' was his slogan."[33] Rosenwald created and was active in the Rosenwald Fund, which built the Chicago Museum of Science and Industry, assisted Jewish causes, and supplied major contributions for 22 YMCAs/YWCAs. The Fund, however, is best known for its contributions to the education and health of African Americans. "By 1932, the year Julius died, an astonishing 4,977 Rosenwald schools, and 380 complementary buildings, had been erected in every Southern locale with a significant black population. Fully 35 percent of all black children in the South (and 27 percent of black children period) were educated that year in a Rosenwald school."[34]

1914, Frederick H. Goff—Frederick H. Goff and the City of

Cleveland developed a love affair. Cleveland Mayor Frederick Kohler stated, "He was the one man in whom all classes of people had absolute faith."[35] Frederick Goff, Cleveland Trust Company President, "convinced the Cleveland Trust board to adopt a Resolution and Declaration of Trust creating the Cleveland Foundation" in 1914.[36] Thus, the Cleveland Foundation became the world's first community foundation. Goff's concept was to create a "community trust" that would combine the resources of the community's philanthropists and distributed the interest generated from their gifts for the benefit of the community. His efforts brought lasting change to Cleveland. "From their beginnings in Cleveland in 1914, community foundations have now expanded around the globe, and now are a major force in philanthropy worldwide."[37] Frederick Goff is the reason so many million dollar moments have been created.

1916-1926, Edward Drummond Libbey—Considered the father of the glass industry in Toledo, Ohio, Edward Drummond Libbey owned The Libbey Glass Company. He died in 1925 and left a $1 million endowment to the Toledo Museum of Art. He had founded the Museum in 1901 and served as its first Chairman of the Board. The success of his company and the prestige of the Toledo Museum of Art went hand-in-hand. Rising costs inspired Libbey to pledge $400,000 for an endowment if the public would raise the same. The fundraising was successful. Due to World War I and later economic depression, the Museum's expansion, planned in 1916, was not completed until 1926, but did so thanks to another Libbey gift of $850,000. Other important contributions by the Museum's founder included his prestigious art and glass collections.[38]

1932-1934, John D. Rockefeller, Jr.—Following in the footsteps of his father, John D. Rockefeller, Sr., could not have been easy for John D. Rockefeller, Jr., however he was able to make his own mark in philanthropic circles. "His principal philanthropic interests included conserving natural landscapes, preserving historical landmarks, collecting fine art, fostering international cooperation, and promoting the cause of Protestant Modernism."[39] His gifts to conservation efforts may have drawn the most press, but the *New York Times* seemed to be fascinated with another philanthropic effort. "Junior," as he was known, donated land on York Avenue for a new Memorial Hospital location. The land was valued at $900,000. Two years later, he granted Memorial Hospital $3 million for a move across town. Memorial Hospital officially reopened at the new location in 1939.[40] Memorial was later renamed the Memorial Sloan Kettering Cancer Center.

1937, Eli Lilly—In the same way that Eli Lilly was instrumental in developing insulin to treat diabetes and combating polio, Lilly was a game changer in the world of philanthropy, especially to the children's museum, private religious groups who helped the poor and needy children, and Earlham and Wabash Colleges.[41] "Along with his father and brother, Eli Lilly founded the Lilly Endowment, comprised of Lilly stock and closely controlled by the Lilly family. It is still one of the largest philanthropies in the country. The Lilly Endowment is notable for its support of community-service organizations in Indiana and its unusual portfolio of religious giving, including support for scholars working on religious topics and financial aid to divinity and theology students. The Lilly Endowment has made more than $5 billion in grants since 1937.[42]

1937, Andrew Mellon—Like Andrew Carnegie, Andrew Mellon gained prominence in the Pittsburgh, Pennsylvania area. A financier, his early contributions supported the University of Pittsburgh and what was to become Carnegie-Mellon University. One of the nation's foremost art collectors, Mellon gave a collection valued at $25 million to the U.S. government in 1937. Among other paintings, it contained Raphael's *Alba Madonna*, 23 Rembrandts, and six Vermeers. Mellon donated $15 million to build the National Gallery of Art to house the collection. The museum opened n 1941.[43] For good measure, Carnegie gifted $5 million of pink Tennessee marble for the construction of this unique edifice.

1945, Alford P. Sloan—Alford P. Sloan helped make General Motors a car manufacturing giant. He oversaw car advances such as four-wheel brakes, ethyl gasoline, crankcase ventilation, and knee-action front springs.[44] Henry Ford, II, said Sloan, was, "one of a handful of men who actually made automotive history."[45] The Chairman of General Motors, Sloan, donated $4 million to create the Sloan-Kettering Institute for Cancer Research through his Sloan Foundation. Charles F. Kettering, GM's vice president and director of research, agreed to oversee the organization of a cancer research program based on industrial techniques. The initially independent research institute was built adjacent to Memorial Hospital. Beyond his individual acts of philanthropy, he created the Alford P. Sloan Foundation in the mid-1930s which has helped make engineering advances possible at institutions such as MIT and the California Institute of Technology.

1953-1976, Howard Hughes—Due to his wealth, eccentric ways, and reclusiveness, Howard Hughes was one of the most interesting figures in American business.[46] In 1951, Hughes personally funded six physician-scientists and appointed them as Howard Hughes Medical Research Fellows. Two years later, he chartered the Howard Hughes Medical Institute (HHMI) in Delaware, and he became the Institute's sole Trustee. The charter stated that "the primary purpose and objective of the Howard Hughes Medical Institute shall be the promotion of human knowledge within the field of the basic sciences (principally the field of medical research and medical education) and the effective application thereof for the benefit of mankind." The HHMI's funding of research remained modest, but steady, up until the time of Hughes' death in 1976. In 1985, the HHMI Board of Trustees sold the Hughes Aircraft Company (the major source of funding for the HHMI) to General Motors Corporation; thus, establishing a $5 billion endowment for the Institute, and making it one of the largest philanthropies in America.

1979, Sam Walton—A graduate of the University of Missouri and an Army veteran, Sam Walton founded Walmart in 1962. Walton had a strong belief in giving back to society. The Walmart Foundation (now The Walmart Family Foundation) was established in 1979 to contribute to the underprivileged, focusing on the core areas of opportunity, sustainability, and community. "Sam and wife Helen were... generous personally. They donated $6 million to the Presbyterian Church, started a program that allowed students in Central Arkansas to study at Arkansas colleges... donated funds (in

Bentonville) that, among other things, upgrade the library, build a recreation center, and support a fine arts center."[47] Sam Walton's legacy lives on through the Walmart Family Foundation. Of the $454.4 million in grants made by the Walton Family Foundation in 2016, Northwest Arkansas received the bulk of the home region grants: $41.5 million.[48] Today, the Walmart Family Foundation "is focused in three areas: systemic reform of primary education (K-12); the environment, specifically marine and freshwater conservation; and the foundation's home region of Northwest Arkansas and the delta region of Arkansas and Mississippi."[49]

1979, Conrad Hilton—Long before Conrad Hilton became one of the most recognizable figures in American society, he ran his father's general store, served his country in World War I, and was twice elected to the New Mexico legislature. These experiences helped him build a hotel empire.[50] He created the Conrad Hilton Foundation in 1944 to "relieve the suffering, the distressed, and the destitute; shelter little children with the umbrella of your charity; support the Catholic Sisters, who devote their love and life's work for the good of mankind; let there be no territorial, religious, or other color restrictions on your benefactions; and assist noble goals into specific, practical actions."[51]

Conrad "Hilton was generous to charitable health-care providers, both Catholic and non-Catholic. He led the capital campaign for St. John's Health Center in Santa Monica, California. In 1972, Hilton committed $10 million to build a research center at the Mayo Clinic."[52]

Conrad Hilton left virtually his entire estate to the Foundation. The value of the estate was $100 million.[53]

1981-present, George Soros—George Soros is known as a financial and economic genius, and his philanthropy has produced remarkable results. Examples of his generosity include major donations to the International Crisis Group and UNICEF, giving each $5 million, and in early 2016, he donated $4 million to the University of Connecticut's Human Rights Institute.[54] Since he retired from actively making money, Soros has worked on giving it away. *Forbes* estimated the self-made billionaire has a net worth of $24.2 billion, and he has given away nearly half that amount since he began his philanthropic efforts in the 1970s.

Born in 1930, Soros lived through the Nazi occupation of his birth country, and would later immigrate to the United States where his financial wizardry made him a billionaire.

1982, Paul Newman—Cleveland is the home of the community foundation, United Way, and Paul Newman. A stint in the United States Navy helped him find direction in life before graduating from Kenyon College. But, it was at Yale's School of Drama where Paul Newman was discovered. Beyond his movie career, Newman played jazz piano, was active in democratic politics, and owned Newman-Haas Auto Racing. Living his quote, "A man can only be judged by his actions, and not by his good intentions or his beliefs," Newman formed Newman's Own Foundation. A private foundation created in 2005, its purpose is to sustain the legacy of Newman's philanthropic work. Funded entirely through the profits and royalties of Newman's Own products, the Foundation does not maintain an endowment, raise funds, or accept donations.[55] Since 1982, when Newman first declared, "Let's give it all away," more than $495 million has been donated to thousands of nonprofit organizations helping people in need around the world. More than 600 grants, totaling $27.3 million, were made by the Foundation in 2016.

The 2000s

2002, Eddie C. Brown—Eddie C. Brown earned college degrees from Howard University, New York University, and the Indiana University Kelley School of Business before he founded Baltimore-based Brown Capital Management in 1983. Brown Capital Management is one of the America's oldest African-American-owned investment-management firms. He and his wife established the Eddie C. and C. Sylvia Brown Family Foundation at the Baltimore Community Foundation in 1994. In 2002, the couple donated $5 million to the Baltimore Public School system, starting the Turning the Corner Achievement Program, an initiative which prepares African-American middle-school students in Baltimore for high school and beyond.[56]

2003, Joan Kroc—Joan Kroc inherited the vast fortune of Ray Kroc, the legendary head of McDonald's. Her posthumous $235 million gift to National Public Radio (NPR) is credited with putting the network on sound financial footing, and her $2 billion gift to the Salvation Army created several dozen world-class recreation facilities in poor neighborhoods around the country.[57] An *Inside Philanthropy* article mused, "There wasn't one, but scattershot clues to her unorthodox philanthropy could be found in news articles: centers for the study of peace named for her on the campuses at Notre Dame and the University of San Diego. Recreation centers funded by a far larger bequest than the one to NPR. Her $1.6 billion to the Salvation Army, named for both her and her husband. Flood relief funds to the tune of $15 million during the devastation in Grand Forks in 1997, which she'd given anonymously—until a wily reporter traced the tail number of her private jet and outed her as the 'angel.'"[58]

2006-2017, Warren Buffett—In 2006 Warren Buffet announced he would give 85 percent of his fortune to charitable organizations. The 85 percent figure has since been revised to 99 percent. Known as the Oracle of Omaha, and the creator of Berkshire-Hathaway, Buffett is considered as one of the finest investment minds of our generation, and has the wealth to prove it. In less than eleven years, Buffett has given $27.54 billion to charitable efforts, including $3.17 billion of Berkshire-Hathaway Class B Stock in 2017 to five foundations. Those five foundations include: the Bill & Melinda Gates Foundation, Susan Thompson Buffett Foundation, Sherwood Foundation, Howard G. Buffett Foundation, and NoVo Foundation.[59] His philosophy on philanthropy is simple, "If you're in the luckiest 1 percent of humanity, you owe it to the rest of humanity to think about the other 99 percent."

2013-Present, Bill and Melinda Gates—Bill Gates is synonymous with Microsoft, wealth, and charity. Melinda Gates joined forces with her husband, for many years the richest individual in the America, to form the Bill and Melinda Gates Foundation in 2000. Their impact on the world of philanthropy has been monumental, but no more important is their efforts to eradicate polio throughout the world. "On June 12, 2017, Bill & Melinda Gates Foundation announced a commitment of up to $450 million to support the eradication of polio. This expanded agreement will translate into $450 million for polio eradication activities, including immunization and surveillance over the next three years. This funding extension reaffirms a commitment established at the 2013 Rotary Convention in Lisbon, Portugal, when the Gates Foundation pledged to match Rotary contributions two-to-one, up to $35 million per year through 2018."[60]

2015, Mark Zuckerberg and Priscilla Chan, MD—Mark Zuckerberg, like Bill Gates, is a Harvard drop-out. And, like Gates, at a very early age, Zuckerberg has accumulated wealth beyond imagination. A lightning rod of conversation, Zuckerberg is the CEO of Facebook. Both he and wife, Dr. Priscilla Chan, are in their early thirties. In December 2015, the Zuckerbergs announced the birth of their daughter Max, and, at the same time, pledged to donate 99 percent of their Facebook shares, then valued at $45 billion, to the Chan Zuckerberg Initiative, their new charitable foundation with focuses on health and education. The donation will not be given to charity immediately, but over the course of their lives.[61] "Our goals for the future center on two ideas: advancing human potential and promoting equal opportunity. We want to push the boundaries of how great a human life can be and make sure that everyone has access to these opportunities regardless of their circumstances."[62]

BONUS CHAPTER
Not So Frequent Million Dollar Moments

Million-dollar gifts are transformational. In 2008, Terry Burton wrote: "Transformational gifts are fast becoming nonprofits' equivalent of the holy grail. It seems as though not a week passes without news of another extraordinary gift delivered to the doorstep of one of America's million plus nonprofits."

In decades past, such gifts were most often directed to a select few institutions of higher education such as Harvard, Yale, and Princeton. But contemporary philanthropists, flush with new wealth earned during and subsequent to the dot com boom of the 1990s, are choosing a wider array of beneficiaries.

For those charities privileged enough to receive a transformational gift, the impact is stunning. A budget deficit might disappear. A brand might be suddenly poised for a turn. Creditability with other donors may zoom to new levels. Certainly, long-term plans for service delivery can be surrounded by a new blanket of financial security and certainty.

Yes, there is hope for nonprofits whose names are not Harvard, Yale, or Princeton to attract million-dollar gifts. According to Coutts, the increased number of million-dollar donations is shared among a growing pool of recipients. The rise in the number of donations in 2015 was, in part, reflected by an increase in the number of organizations benefiting from these gifts. In the UK, the number of distinct beneficiaries rose by nearly ten percent (from 243 to 267) compared to 2014, while in the US the increase was even more marked, at 64 percent (from 724 to 1,189). The growth in the number of recipients of million-dollar donations is a positive sign regarding the breadth and variety of charitable activity benefiting from major philanthropy.[63]

Indiana University's Lilly Family School of Philanthropy is the leading source of information on million dollar giving in America. In 2010, Bill and Melinda Gates sought to consolidate existing data on million dollar giving, develop a website, and create a "Million Dollar List." They founded the Million Dollar List, which has become an important prospect research tool for resource development professionals, according to the school's Assistant Director for Research and Partnerships, Jacqueline Ackerman. The 2013 edition of the Million Dollar List details over 1,400 gifts of $1 million or more that were made in the U.S. during 2012. They totaled nearly $14 billion. Almost 1,000 organizations received million-dollar gifts during that period with a mean of $9.9 million and a median of $2.5 million.

More recently, million-dollar contributions to America's nonprofits are on the rise. "The significant growth in million-dollar-plus giving in the U.S. is good news," said Una Osili, PhD, Professor of Economics and Associate Dean for Research and International Programs at the Lilly Family School. "For the first time in eight years, we are seeing giving at this level rebound to where it was before the recession. Donors are increasing their support and dedication to the causes they care about."[64]

Not only are more organizations receiving million-dollar gifts, but more non-traditional nonprofits are attracting their own million-dollar moments. This chapter is devoted to both major names who are generating multiple million-dollar gifts and those who are of the lesser known variety. Major names such as the John F. Kennedy Center, the Robin Hood Foundation, and the Smithsonian National Museum of African American History and Culture are featured, along with a dozen lesser known nonprofits. Included are their mission statements to indicate the diversity of people helped across America by these nonprofits, as well as the donors who helped make said missions come alive.

Major Names, Big-Time Gifts

The John F. Kennedy Center

In 1958, President Dwight D. Eisenhower signed bipartisan legislation creating a National Cultural Center. Thirteen years later, the John F. Kennedy Center for the Performing Arts, located on the banks of the Potomac River near the Lincoln Memorial in Washington, D.C., opened to the public.

According to its mission statement, the center "is committed to increasing opportunities for all people to participate in and understand the arts. To fulfill that mission, the Center strives to commission, produce, and present performances reflecting the highest standards of excellence and diversity indicative of the world in which we live, and to make those performances accessible to the broadest possible audience through arts education."

In 2015, around 80 percent of the nearly 1,200 nonprofit organizations that received gifts of $1 million or more received only one such donation. A small number of organizations received more than one gift. The biggest beneficiary that year, the Kennedy Center for the Performing Arts, received eighteen separate gifts at that level.[65]

Many stories behind these generous gifts are outlined on the Kennedy Center website. Here are four examples:

"I Am So Grateful for What the Arts Have Done for Me." ... One of the greatest evenings I've ever experienced was forging my way through a snowstorm to the Kennedy Center to see the Mariinsky Ballet perform Sleeping Beauty," Jane said. It was a magical performance—the whole experience was like a fairytale… No other venue in the United States presents as many of the world's major ballet companies each year as the Kennedy Center. Truly a national treasure!

Jane Bergnerb
Harvard Law Graduate

"I want to leave a legacy that reflects my values and beliefs."…There is nothing I won't do for the Kennedy Center. When I volunteer, I do it without conditions…The Kennedy Center is not just any institution— it serves as a place for the spirit. When I have a tough day at work I come to the Kennedy Center, and right away my spirits are lifted and I feel reenergized, he explains….He likes to paraphrase President John F. Kennedy by saying, 'Ask not what the Kennedy Center can do for you; ask what you can do for the Kennedy Center.'

Bill Turner, PhD
former English Professor

"Everyone needs art in their lives." Bob adds, "it's what keeps a community vibrant"… Since arriving in Washington DC in 1975, they have been regulars at the Kennedy Center, attending a wide variety of performances, but reserve a special place in their hearts for Washington National Opera productions. Jamie was a founding member of the Women's Committee of the Opera in 1976; Bob joined the WNO Board in 1980, serving as General Counsel for the majority of his term, and as President for four years …We feel it's important to support the performances too, so they will be here for our grandchildren and for generations to come.

Bob and Jamie Craft, former President
Washington National Opera Productions

"The arts saved my life." … When Dr. James T. Jackson first moved to Washington, DC, in 2001, he would walk from his new office at George Washington University to the Kennedy Center every day after work to clear his mind and renew his spirit. "DC is a hard place, especially if you don't know a lot of people," he says. The Kennedy Center really saved me my first year … I feel that I owe a debt, which is why I wanted to give back to the Kennedy Center by making the Center the beneficiary of my life insurance policies. I want other people to have the opportunities that I had. What really matters is what you want for yourself in life and how you dedicate yourself to achieving it.

Dr. James T. Jackson
Professor,
Curriculum and Instruction, Howard University

The Robin Hood Foundation

The mission of the Robin Hood Foundation is "to improve the living standards for 1.8 million low-income New Yorkers." Established in 1988, Robin Hood is New York's largest poverty-fighting organization and has focused on finding, funding, and creating programs and schools that generate meaningful and measurable results for families in New York's poorest neighborhoods.

Few nonprofit organizations are blessed with the star power of the Robin Hood Foundation. Thanks to a $15 million challenge gift from Ken Griffin, the billionaire founder of hedge fund firm Citadel LLC, the 2017 Robin Hood gala raised $54.5 million to fight New York City poverty. The Foundation, a favorite cause of Wall Street's elite, had involvement from, or attendance by, such luminaries as Alex Rodriguez, Andrew Cuomo, Jeb Bush, Henry Kravis, Dave Chappelle, Michael Douglas, Catherine Zeta-Jones, Jennifer Lopez, and David and Jackie Simon.

National Museum of African-American History and Culture

The mission of the National Museum of African American History and Culture is to "tell the story of America through the lens of black history and culture."

The Museum is a community resource that helps visitors learn about themselves, their histories, and their common cultures. With a gift of $20 million, billionaire philanthropist Robert Smith became the second-highest private donor to the National Museum of African American History and Culture in 2014.[66] Only Oprah Winfrey gave more, $21 million. Robert Smith is Chairman and Chief Executive of

Vista Equity Partners. His philanthropy, whether personal or from the foundation he leads, came with a powerful message to others who have financial capabilities. "…step out there and do more community work—real work, not just going to a boys and girls club and writing a $10,000 check and going to a gala,"… "We want to create an environment for these young people that will help them become their best selves."[67]

Emerging Names with Million-Dollar Moments

Miami Lighthouse for the Blind and Visually Impaired

Established in 1931, the mission statement of the Miami Lighthouse for the Blind and Visually Impaired is "to provide vision rehabilitation and eye health services that promote independence, to collaborate with and educate professionals, and to conduct research in related fields."

In 2015, on the group's 85th anniversary, The Braman Family Foundation pledged $1 million to the charity. The Foundation was created by Norman Braman, high-end automobile dealer and former Owner of the NFL's Philadelphia Eagles. The Foundation's gift will be utilized for the new Miami Lighthouse Center of Excellence for Visually Impaired Children, specifically for a pre-kindergarten for blind three and four year-olds and an early intervention center for blind babies.

Colby College

According to Colby College's mission and precepts statement, the school:

"is committed to the belief that the best preparation for life, and especially for the professions that require specialized study, is a broad acquaintance with human knowledge. The Colby experience is designed to enable each student to find and fulfill his or her own unique potential. It is hoped that students will become critical and imaginative thinkers who are welcoming of diversity and compassionate toward others, capable of distinguishing fact from opinion, intellectually curious and aesthetically aware, adept at synthesis as well as analysis, broadly educated with depth in some areas, proficient in writing and speaking, familiar with one or more scientific disciplines, knowledgeable about American and other cultures, able to create and enjoy opportunities for lifelong learning, willing to assume leadership roles as students and citizens, prepared to respond flexibly to the changing demands of the world of work, useful to society, and happy with themselves."

Colby College is the center of intellectual engagement for the community of Waterville, Maine. Its student body numbers approximately 1,800. At the hub of this liberal arts institution is its Colby Museum of Art. Peter Lunder graduated from Colby College in 1956, and was President of Dexter Shoe Company. He and wife Paula have both received honorary degrees from Colby, and have a history of support for nonprofits such as the Smithsonian American Art Museum, the Dana Farber Foundation, and Maine College of Art. The Lunders contributed a major portion of their valuable art collection, valued at over $100 million, to Colby in 2007, along with a cash gift which was directed to care for the collection. Beyond these acts of kindness, the Lunders also supported the building of a pavilion to house the collection; thus, making it the largest museum in the state of Maine.[68] The gift stemmed from his connection to the school, and he and his wife's desire to make the Lunder collection accessible to Colby College and all residents of Waterville.[69]

Mercersburg Academy

The mission of Mercersburg Academy, Franklin County, Pennsylvania, is to prepare "young men and women from diverse backgrounds for college and for life in a global community. Students at Mercersburg pursue a rigorous and dynamic curriculum while learning to live together harmoniously in a supportive residential environment. Mercersburg's talented faculty instill in students the value of hard work and the importance of character and community as they teach students to think for themselves, to approach life thoughtfully and creatively, to thrive physically, to act morally, to value the spiritual dimension of human existence, and to serve others."

Why make a gift of $100 million to a school of 330 students? Deborah Simon spent two years at Mercersburg Academy Franklin County, Pennsylvania before attending the University of Southern California. Today she is the President of the Mercersburg Board of Regents. According to Deborah, "I want the Mercersburg of the future to be state of the art for the students as far as access to financial aid, teacher endowments, and the things of that nature. I want it to continue to be the best boarding school it can be without losing its ethos of community, integrity, and learning."[70] In 2017, four years after making her transformational gift, Deborah's devotion to Mercersburg grew even stronger. She was named president of the school's Board of Regents. Not only was Deborah the first alumna to make a million dollar gift to Mercersburg, but she has also provided leadership and support to entities such as the Simon Youth Foundation, the Children's Museum of Indianapolis, the Indianapolis Zoological Society, Inc., and the Statue of Liberty-Ellis Island Foundation. Deborah's father, the late Melvin Simon, along with his brothers Herb and Fred, founded what would become Simon Property Group. Her 2013 gift to Mercersburg is the second largest gift ever made to an independent school in the US, according to school officials.

DeYor Performing Arts Center

The home of the Youngstown Symphony Orchestra, the mission statement of the DeYor Performing Arts Center is brief, and to the point: "Music education is the cornerstone of our mission."

There was a time when Youngstown, Ohio was alive and thriving, thanks to a booming steel industry and to the success of Edward J. DeBartolo, Sr. in the shopping center business. Today, not so much.

Who would have thought that the National Football League's San Francisco 49ers would be owned by a woman residing in Youngstown? That woman is Denise DeBartolo York, and her generosity is multifold.

According to Joanne Pasternack, Vice President and Executive Director, Community Relations and the San Francisco 49ers Foundation:

"Denise DeBartolo York has been a wonderful mentor and someone I greatly admire. After I graduated law school and before I came to the 49ers, I worked with Special Olympics. Eunice Kennedy Shriver, who founded Special Olympics, was a huge mentor in my life. I learned so much from being around her and simply conversing with her. One quote that described Mrs. Shriver perfectly—and I wear it engraved on a bracelet— is from Shakespeare—'Though she be but little, she is fierce.' Both Denise and Eunice demonstrated a tremendous capacity to make things happen and to find a way to make the world a better place. Because I have had the ability to learn from them directly and to see the impact of their commitment to front-line philanthropy, I am continuously inspired every day."[71]

What greater compliment can an individual receive? Far from San Francisco, Denise has always made sure that Youngstown, and surrounding suburbs, is endowed with a wonderful quality of life, especially in the area of education. She is a champion of those at-risk, in need, and without financial aid, as well as her alma mater, Cardinal Mooney High School.

In 2006, Denise and husband, Dr. John York, made a game-changing gift in the form of a $1 million contribution to create the DeYor Center. Formerly known as the Youngstown Symphony Center, Denise and John stated, "We are pleased to help enhance the Youngstown Symphony Center and look forward to everyone working together to return our downtown area to its former vibrancy."[72] It was the icing on the cake for desperately needed renovation and expansion of the arts facility.

The Boys & Girls Clubs of the Gulf Coast

The mission statement of the Boys & Girls Clubs of the Gulf Coast is "to enable all young people, especially those who need us most, to reach their full potential as productive, caring, responsible citizens."

It is a name that will not be forgotten. Katrina. It evokes memories of destruction and death. Although Louisiana bore the brunt of Hurricane Katrina's wrath in 2005, Mississippi was not spared. Katrina devastated all five facilities of the Boys & Girls Clubs of the Gulf Coast. Many people came to the aid of the Boys & Girls Clubs, but no individual was more generous than golf course designer Tom Fazio. Tom and his wife already had an emotional stake in the Boy & Girls Clubs as they founded the Boys & Girls Club of Henderson County. His gift of $1 million was the largest contribution by an individual in a $19 million effort to rebuild the five facilities. The five were fully functional by 2010.[73]

Greater Ozarks-Arkansas Red Cross

The American Red Cross shelters, feeds, and provides emotional support to victims of disasters, supplies about 40 percent of the nation's blood, teaches skills that save lives, provides international humanitarian aid, and supports military members and their families.

Tornadoes take a heavy toll on the central plains states every year in America. On May 22, 2011, disaster struck the area served by the Greater Ozarks-Arkansas Red Cross. That day the city of Joplin, Missouri was devastated by an EF-5 tornado. It killed 158 and injured over 1,000 people. At one point the twister was a mile wide with winds in excess of 200 miles per hour. It was on the ground for just over 22 miles and destroyed 7,000 homes and scores of businesses and public buildings.[74]

Three days later, a check for $1 million was presented to the Greater Ozarks-Arkansas Red Cross by David Humphreys, President and CEO of TAMKO Building Products, Inc. "This is about individuals and businesses helping however they can help," he said. "We thought it was important to do something, and to do it early and now."[75] TAMKO's manufacturing and administrative operations are centered in the Joplin area. Mr. Humphreys went on to say that, "many of the company's 800 or so employees or their family members have lost their homes or been otherwise affected by the storm."[76]

The Salvation Army Center of Hope

The mission of the Salvation Army is to preach the gospel of Jesus Christ and to meet human needs in His name without discrimination.

When Hurricane Harvey struck the State of Texas in 2017, it wreaked devastation to everything in its path. Fortunately for the residents of Temple, Texas, the Salvation Army Center of Hope was prepared to help in a big way. One year earlier, the organization completed a $4.9 million campaign to build a 22,000 square foot facility which would provide "emergency shelter, food and rehabilitation all under one roof."[77] The most impactful gift in that effort was $1 million from Drayton and Elizabeth McLane.

When ground was broken in June 2013, the effort was renamed the Salvation Army McLane Center of Hope. The McLane Center became the first Bell County homeless shelter, the only one found between Waco and Austin, and had the capacity to accommodate up to 100 participants at a time.[78] Drayton McLane is the former owner of Major League Baseball's Houston Astros. Drayton McLane turned his family's grocery distribution company, McLane Co., into an international firm and sold it to Walmart for $50 million and 10.4 million shares of Walmart.

Carver IDEA (Individuals Dedicated to Excellence and Achievement)

According to its mission statement, "The Carver Academy offers elementary-age children a challenging academic program featuring small classes, leadership opportunities, and a nurturing family-like environment based upon the foundation of Judeo-Christian scripture. Graduates of The Carver Academy will be prepared for success in the nation's most competitive high schools and will display the highest levels of leadership, discipline, initiative and integrity. The Carver Academy welcomes all children regardless of race, creed or financial status."

The Carver School, San Antonio, Texas, would not exist if it weren't for David Robinson. Beloved in San Antonio as a member of the National Basketball Association Champion San Antonio Spurs and two-time Olympic Gold Medalist in basketball, he sought to develop an educational center where multicultural students would face stringent academic challenges and seek success at the highest level.[79] His pledge of $9 million helped build the Carver Academy in 1997 and create an endowment for the school when it opened its doors in 2001.[80]

The mission statement of Carver IDEA is "public schools prepare students from underserved communities for success in college and citizenship."

Tom Torkelson and JoAnn Gama founded the IDEA Academy as an after school program in Donna, Texas, in 1998. It was created as a way to help combat some of the major educational deficiencies they saw in their students, focusing the program on student achievement and college readiness. It grew into a charter school powerhouse in the state of Texas with 100 percent of its graduates achieving college acceptance. IDEA schools operate outside of independent school districts, but do receive state and federal funds, and are held accountable through state testing requirements. Student enrollment is free, but transportation is not provided by IDEA schools.

Carver Academy remained private until 2012. According to its founder, "I first partnered with IDEA in 2012 because I saw the district's results firsthand. IDEA was—and still is—ensuring that 100 percent of its senior class each year is accepted to a college or university. This public school system is proving the transformational power of an excellent pre-college education. Each child in Texas deserves an education like that."[81]

Phelps County Community Foundation

The Mission of the Phelps County Community Foundation is "to encourage and provide opportunities for charitable giving, to manage and distribute the funds in a responsible manner, and to enhance the quality of life for the people of Phelps County."

Million-dollar magic can happen even in the smallest of communities or in the most remote locations. Such is the story of LeonaBelle Kipp and the Phelps County Community Foundation of Holdrege, Nebraska.

"In May of 2011, the Foundation was advised that it would receive a gift through LeonaBelle's estate. At that time, we could not have imagined that this gift would be worth $2.6 Million. LeonaBelle established the Ivan and LeonaBelle Kipp Scholarship Fund in 2004 to benefit graduating seniors from the Bertrand Senior High School … We were honored and pleased that LeonaBelle thought enough of the Foundation's work to leave this gift to us."[82] Ivan and LeonaBelle Kipp lived on rural Nebraska farms, growing corn and raising cattle, for the first 40 years of their marriage.

The University of North Dakota

The University of North Dakota "serves the state, the country, and the world community through teaching, research, creative activities, and service. State-assisted, the University's work depends also on federal, private, and corporate sources. With other research universities, the University shares a distinctive responsibility for the discovery, development, preservation, and dissemination of knowledge. Through its sponsorship and encouragement of basic and applied research, scholarship, and creative endeavor, the University contributes to the public well-being."

Just how big is the impact of the oil boom on North Dakota? According to *Inside Climate News*, it is transformational. "Oil development has transformed this state to the point where it's hard to find a place or person that hasn't been touched by the boom. Energy companies have drilled more than 8,000 wells into western North Dakota's rugged prairie since the beginning of 2010, quadrupling the state's oil production. From July 2011 through June 2013, the state collected $4 billion in oil taxes, and is expecting a $1 billion surplus for the current biennium, not including an oil-funded sovereign wealth fund that will approach a balance of $3 billion."[83] One of the major beneficiaries of this economic windfall is the University of North Dakota. "In June, the University of North Dakota announced a $5 million gift from the company (Hess Corp) that will pay for three new high-tech laboratories at its College of Engineering and Mines, with each lab sporting Hess's name. Right next door is the university's Harold Hamm School of Geology and Geological Engineering, a renaming of its geology department announced in 2012 after Continental and Hamm, the company's CEO, donated $10 million to the school."[84]

Torrance (California) Memorial Medical Center

The Torrance Memorial Medical Center is a locally governed, 446-bed, nonprofit medical center, "the purpose of which is to provide quality healthcare services, predominantly to the residents of the South Bay, Peninsula and Harbor communities of Los Angeles County. Under the governance of a community-based Board of Trustees, Torrance Memorial services the public interest by improving the community health within the scope and expertise of its resources; offering the most current and effective medical technologies rendered in a compassionate, caring manner; and maintaining long-term stability in order to assure its strength and viability for the benefit of the community.

Located in the South Bay area of Los Angeles County, Torrance, California, has a population of nearly 150,000. Within an easy drive of Torrance are centers of medical excellence such as UCLA Medical Center, Cedars-Sinai Medical Center, Hoag Memorial Medical Presbyterian, Huntington Memorial Hospital, and the University of Southern California's Keck Hospital.

Not everyone wants to make the trip to other hospitals in the region, especially Melanie and Richard Lundquist. Mrs. Lundquist stated, "It dawned on me about twenty years ago that if I had a heart attack at 4 p.m. in the afternoon I was DOA if I had to go to Cedars… Top-notch care should not depend on your ZIP Code."[85] Thus, earlier contributions of $18 million and $50 million brought about the Lundquist Cardiovascular Institute and the Lundquist (patient) Tower at Torrance Memorial Medical Center.[86] Palos Verdes Estates residents Melanie and Richard Lundquist donated $32 million to Torrance Memorial Medical Center in 2017 to improve neurological, orthopedic, and spinal care in the hospital. The gift…brings the couple's total contributions to the hospital to $100 million over the last 11 years. Melanie volunteered at the Hospital's front desk for more than a decade.[87]

INDEX

ENDNOTES

[1]Davison, Joanne, "Happy Campers," *The Denver Post* (February 22, 2010).

[2]Causey, Caitlin, "Nonprofit Spotlight: Roundup River Ranch Lets Sick Kids Feel Like Kids," *Post Independent* (May 29, 2017).

[3]Ibid.

[4]Tempel, Eugene, Timothy Seiler, and Dwight Burlingame, eds., *Achieving Excellence in Fundraising* (Hoboken: John Wiley & Sons, 2016), 3-10.

[5]Osili, Una, Chelsea Clark, Mallory St. Claire, Jonathan Bergdoll, "The 2016 U.S. Trust Study of High Net Worth Philanthropy," (Indianapolis: Indiana University Lilly Family School of Philanthropy, 2016), http://hdl.handle.net/1805/11234.

[6]Tempel, 5.

[7]Ibid.

[8]"Remembering Bobby Fong, Former Butler President," *Indianapolis Monthly* (September 10, 2014), https://www.indianapolismonthly.com/news-opinion/butler-university-president-bobby-fong-dies/.

[9]Coutts Institute, "Million Dollar Donor Report: United States," (2016), http://philanthropy.coutts.com/en/reports/2016/united-states/findings.html.

[10]"GivingUSA 2017: The Annual Report on Philanthropy for the Year 2016," *GivingUSA*, (June 12, 2017), https://store.givingusa.org/collections/2017-products.

[11]Brubacher, John and Willis Rudy, *Higher Education in Transition: A History of American Colleges and Universities,* 3rd ed. (New York: Routledge, 1976), 377.

[12]Biondolillo, Steven, "The Father of Philanthropy," *The Wall Street Journal* (January 2, 1997).

[13]"Stephen Girard," The Almanac of American Philanthropy, Philanthropy Roundtable, https://www.philanthropyroundtable.org/almanac/stephen-girard.

[14]Feldberg, Michael, *Blessings of Freedom: Chapters in American Jewish History* (Hoboken: Ktav Publishing House, 2002).

[15]Nash, Merle, and Roderick Curti, *Philanthropy in the Shaping of American Higher Education* (New Brunswick: Rutgers University Press, 1965).

[16]"'I Would Found an Institution': The Ezra Cornell Bicentennial," Cornell University, 2006, http://rmc.library.cornell.edu/ezra/exhibition/founding/index.html.

[17]Ibid.

[18]Ibid.

[19]"Readers: Black History Month Fact of the Day – The Peabody Fund for Black Education in the South Established," Chocolate Vent, February 6, 2014, https://chocolatevent.com/tag/peabody/.

[20]"History of Vanderbilt University," Vanderbilt, 2016, https://www.vanderbilt.edu/about/history/.

[21]Ibid.

[22]Carnegie, Andrew, "The Best Fields for Philanthropy," *The North American Review* 149, no. 1 (July 1889): 682-698.

[23]Grossman, Ron, "The University of Chicago Opens," *Chicago Tribune*, accessed October 3, 2018, http://www.chicagotribune.com/news/nationworld/politics/chi-chicagodays-universitychicago-story-story.html.

[24]Ibid.

[25]Chesney, AM, *The Johns Hopkins Hospital and the Johns Hopkins University School of Medicine: A Chronicle*, vol. 1, 1867-1893 (1943), https://www.ncbi.nlm.nih.gov/pmc/articles/PMC3012286/#B1.

[26]"Higher Education: Notable Contributions to Higher Education from the Philanthropy Hall of Fame," *Philanthropy*, Winter 2013, https://www.philanthropyroundtable.org/philanthropy-magazine/article/higher-education.

[27]"Andrew Carnegie," *Philanthropy Roundtable*, The Almanac of American Philanthropy, 2018, https://www.philanthropyroundtable.org/almanac/andrew-carnegie.

[28]"Andrew Carnegie Biography: Entrepreneur, Business Leader, Philanthropist (1835-1919)," Biography.com, (April 2, 2014), https://www.biography.com/people/andrew-carnegie-9238756.

[29]"George Eastman Biography: Inventor (1854-1932)," Biography.com, (April 2, 2014), https://www.biography.com/people/george-eastman-9283428.

[30]Scott, Eric L., "Eastman, George," *Learning to Give*, accessed October 3, 2018, https://www.learningtogive.org/resources/eastman-george.

[31]Ibid.

[32]Roberts, Alicia S., "Rosenwald, Julius," *Learning to Give*, accessed October 3, 2018, https://www.learningtogive.org/resources/rosenwald-julius.

[33]Zinsmeister, Karl, *The Almanac of American Philanthropy: 2017 Compact Edition*, (Washington DC: Philanthropy Roundtable, 2017).

[34]Ibid.

[35]"Frederick H. Goff: National Intellectual Treasure," The Cleveland Foundation, Foundation of Change, https://www.clevelandfoundation100.org/foundation-of-change/invention/frederick-goff/.

[36]Ibid.

[37]"2008 Community Foundation Global Status Report," Wings Community Foundation, August 2008.

[38]"Toledo Museum of Art," *American Art Gallery*, accessed October 3, 2018, http://americanartgallery.org/museum/readmore/id/581.

[39]Zinsmeister, "John Rockefeller, Jr."

[40]"Rockefeller Provides $3,000,000 To Build Cancer Hospital Here; Gift of General Education Board to Develop a New Center Near Foot of East 68th St. for Expansion of Memorial Institution to Rank with Finest in the World. Rockefeller Gift to Build Hospital," *The New York Times*, (April 28, 1936), https://www.nytimes.com/1936/04/28/archives/rockefeller-provides-3000000-to-build-cancer-hospital-here-gift-of.html.

[41]Zinsmeister, "Eli Lilly."

[42]Ibid.

[43]Zinsmeister, "Andrew Mellon."

[44]"Alfred P. Sloan Jr. Dead at 90; G.M. Leader and Philanthropist; Alfred P. Sloan Jr., Leader of General Motors, Is Dead at 90," *The New York Times*, (February 18, 1966), https://www.nytimes. com/1966/02/18/archives/alfred-p-sloan-jr-dead-at-90-gm-leader-and-philanthropist-alfred-p.html.

[45]Ibid.

[46]"Howard Hughes," Philanthropy Roundtable, Philanthropy Hall of Fame, 2018, https://www.philanthropyroundtable.org/almanac/timeline.

[47]Blumenthal, Karen, *Mr. Sam: How Sam Walton Built Walmart and Became America's Richest Man*, (New York: Penguin Books, 2011).

[48]Peacock, Leslie Newell, "Walton Family Foundation Giving in 2016: $454.4 Million," *Arkansas Times*, (May 23, 2017), https://www. arktimes.com/ArkansasBlog/archives/2017/05/23/walton-family-foundation-giving-in-2016-4544-million.

[49]Walmart Corporation, "About Us," Walton Family Foundation, accessed October 3, 2018, https://www.waltonfamilyfoundation.org/about-us.

[50]Zinsmeister, "Conrad Hilton."

[51]"A History of Hilton Family Philanthropy," Conrad N. Hilton Foundation, accessed October 3, 2018, https://www.hiltonfoundation. org/about/history.

[52]"Conrad Hilton's Estate Is Valued at $100 Million in Court Papers," *New York Times*, (January 17, 1979), https://www.nytimes. com/1979/01/17/archives/conrad-hiltons-estate-is-valued-at-100-million-in-court-papers.html.

[53]"A History of Hilton Family Philanthropy."

[54]Merritt, Grace, "Largest Human Rights Gift to UConn to Provide Scholarships, Build Endowment," University of Connecticut, (January 14, 2016), https://www.foundation.uconn.edu/2016/01/14/largest-human-rights-gift-to-uconn/.

[55]Newman's Own Corporation, "About Us: The Power of Philanthropy," Newman's Own Foundation, accessed October 3, 2018, http://newmansownfoundation.org/about-us/.

⁵⁶"Eddie C. Brown," Black Entrepreneur Profile, accessed October 3, 2018, https://www.blackentrepreneurprofile.com/profile-full/article/eddie-c-brown/.

⁵⁷Napoli, Lisa, "Meet the Woman Who Gave Away the McDonald's Founder's Fortune," *Time*, (December 22, 2016), http://time.com/4616956/mcdonalds-founder-ray-kroc-joan-kroc/.

⁵⁸"Joan Kroc's Radical and Ecstatic Philanthropy," HistPhil, (December 2, 2016), https://histphil.org/2016/12/02/joan-krocs-radical-and-ecstatic-philanthropy/.

⁵⁹Carrig, David, "Warren Buffet Gave away this Much of His Wealth in the Past 10 Years," CNBC, (July 13, 2017), https://www.cnbc.com/2017/07/13/warren-buffett-gave-away-this-much-of-his-wealth-in-the-past-10-years.html.

⁶⁰"Rotary and the Bill & Melinda Gates Foundation Announce $450 Million Commitment to End Polio," *Rotary*, (June 12, 2017), https://www.rotary.org/en/press-release-gates-and-rotary-announce-450-million-commitment-end-polio.

⁶¹Seetharaman, Deepa and Anupreeta Das, "Mark Zuckerberg and Priscilla Chan to Give 99% of Facebook Shares to Charity," *The Wall Street Journal*, (December 2, 2015), https://www.wsj.com/articles/mark-zuckerberg-priscilla-chan-to-give-99-of-facebook-stock-to-philanthropy-1449005878.

⁶²The Chan Zuckerberg Initiative, 2018, https://www.chanzuckerberg.com/.

⁶³Hrywna, Mark, "$1 Million-Plus Gifts Reportedly Tripled," *The Nonprofit Times*, (November 29, 2016), http://www.thenonprofittimes.com/news-articles/1-million-plus-gifts-reportedly-tripled/.

⁶⁴Ibid.

⁶⁵Ibid.

⁶⁶Alexander, Keith, "'Who Is this Robert Smith?': A Quiet Billionaire Makes Some Noise with $20 Million Gift to the African American Museum," *The Washington Post*, (September 24, 2016), https://www.washingtonpost.com/national/who-is-this-robert-smith-a-quiet-billionaire-makes-some-noise-with-20-million-gift-to-the-african-american-museum/2016/09/23/547da3a8-6fd0-11e6-8-365-b19e428a975e_story.html?utm_term=.961eed7f7a30.

[67]Ibid.

[68]Gay, Malcolm, "$100 Million Gift Set To Transform Colby College Museum of Art," *The Boston Globe*, (February 3, 2017), https://www.bostonglobe.com/arts/art/2017/02/03/million-gift-set-transform-colby-college-museum-art/B916OI6JAm7TSB7Qg0FjAN/story.html.

[69]Ibid.

[70]"Deborah Simon, '74," *Mercersburg Magazine*, Summer (August 28, 2013): 22-23.

[71]"Joanne Pasternack," *Philanthropy Playmakers*, http://www.philanthropyplaymakers.com/joanne-pasternack.html.

[72]Skolnick, David, "Youngstown Symphony Center Large Gift Leads to Name Change," *The Vindicator*, (July 6, 2005), http://www.vindy.com/news/2005/jul/06/youngstown-symphony-center-large-gift-leads-to/.

[73]O'Neil, Megan, "After Katrina, Boys and Girls Clubs Go from $19-Million Rebuilding to Reality," *The Chronicle of Philanthropy*, (August 13, 2015), https://www.philanthropy.com/article/After-Katrina-BoysGirls/232373.

[74]Wheatley, Katie, "The May 22, 2011 Joplin, Missouri EF5 Tornado," U.S. Tornadoes, (May 22, 2013), https://www.ustornadoes.com/2013/05/22/joplin-missouri-ef5-tornado-may-22-2011/.

[75]Stefanoni, Andra Bryan, "Carthage Senior Class, TAMKO among Donors," *The Joplin Globe*, (May 25, 2011), http://www.joplinglobe.com/news/local_news/carthage-senior-class-tamko-among-donors/article_34e89d0e-84bf-50b1-bcaf-4160eb1f6914.html.

[76]Ibid.

[77]"McLane Family Gives Million Dollar Gift to Temple Salvation Army Center," Central Texas News Now, accessed October 3, 2018, http://www.kxxv.com/story/21989665/mclane-family-gives-million-dollar-gift-to-temple-salvation-army-center.

[78]Pixler, Kierra, "Homeless Shelter Breaks Ground in Temple," *The Belton Journal*, (June 3, 2013), http://beltonjournal.com/homeless-shelter-breaks-ground-in-temple/.

[79]Dimmick, Iris, "David Robinson Scores Big with IDEA Public School," *Rivard Report*, (May 12, 2015), https://therivardreport.com/david-robinson-scores-big-with-idea-public-school/.

[80]"David and Valerie Robinson's Donation Totals $9 Million," San Antonio Spurs News, (May 24, 2002), https://www.nba.com/spurs/news/robinson_donation_020524.html.

[81]McIntire, Erin, "IDEA Public Schools Reports Success amid Questions around Data Reporting," *Education Dive*, (November 5, 2015), https://www.educationdive.com/news/idea-public-schools-reports-success-amid-questions-around-data-reporting/408616/.

[82]Phelps Foundation Newsletter, *The Phelps County Community Foundation*, (Spring/Summer 2012), http://www.phelpsfoundation.org/wp-content/uploads/2012/07/Newsleter_SPRING_12.pdf.

[83]Kusnetz, Nicholas, "How a Sudden Flood of Oil Money Has Transformed North Dakota," *Inside Climate News*, (July 21, 2014), https://insideclimatenews.org/news/20140721/how-sudden-flood-oil-money-has-transformed-north-dakota.

[84]Ibid.

[85]Karlamangla, Soumya, "Torrance Memorial Hospital Receives $32-Million Donation," *Los Angeles Times*, (June 14, 2017), http://www.latimes.com/local/california/la-me-ln-torrance-memorial-donation-20170614-story.html.

[86]Ibid.

[87]Ibid.